*To Ryan
on their Wedding Day,
October 4, 2025
Grampa + Nena*

UNDENOMINATIONAL CHRISTIANITY

Ruth 1:16-17

UNDENOMINATIONAL CHRISTIANITY

J. N. ARMSTRONG

RESOURCE PUBLICATIONS
2205 Benton
Searcy, AR 72143

Copyright © 2002
Resource Publications

Second Printing, 2003
Third Printing, 2022

ISBN: 978-0-945441-70-0

Scripture taken from the American Standard Version, 1901.

Contents

Foreword	7
An Explanation for the Reader	9
About the Author	11
Preface	17

Undenominational Christianity—

1. An Introduction	19
2. Is It Possible?	23
3. Is It Required?	29
4. How Is It Possible?	35
5. What Is It?	45
6. The Only Basis of Union	53
7. Makes Division Impossible	59
8. Saved After Baptism	65
9. Remission of Sins	73
10. Explanation Needless	79
11. Baptism into What?	83
12. Baptized into What?	91
13. Another Fork	97
14. What Is Baptism?	103
15. The Bible Meaning	111

Foreword

Those of us who have been a part of reprinting this treatment of undenominational Christianity by J. N. Armstrong, president of Harding University from 1924 until 1936, have looked upon our respective tasks as great privileges. We have been reminded that many of our thoughts about the Lord's church have been influenced by the mighty efforts that were made years ago by men who loved God and wanted to follow and abide in nothing but His truth as revealed in the Scriptures. Even though they are dead, they continue to speak (Hebrews 11:4) through the long shadows of their influence that reach across the years.

This particular book, even though it is crowned with age,[1] has a profound message for everyone who wants to follow Christ today. It deserves a reading not only by those who are not undenominational Christians, but also by every member of the Lord's church.

The first copy of this work was done by Herald Publishing Company in Cordell, Oklahoma, in 1913.

---

[1] In the interest of the modern reader, some changes have been made from the original edition.

Resource Publications is reprinting it by permission of Armstrong's grandson, Jack Wood Sears, who has freely given of his time and knowledge to assist us in making the reprint a reality.

Special appreciation should be given to Burl Curtis, whose foresight and encouragement have moved the effort on to its conclusion.

Cheryl Schramm, one of our most efficient proofreaders, designers, and assistant editors, has done a tremendous amount of the work of finalizing the copy for the printer.

Susan Cloer, the excellent office manager of the Truth for Today World Mission School, proofed, provided guidance, and gave other assistance for the completion of the project.

The Truth for Today staff has already provided a copy of this reprint for thousands of national preachers in 155 nations of the world. How they will thrill at the sincere plea found on these pages to be "only Christians and Christians only"!

I would invite you to read this little book with no desire other than to find the truth of God. Do not allow the world around you to deter you from becoming and being what God expects of His people. Remember the Bereans:

> ... they received the word with all readiness of mind, examining the Scriptures daily, whether these things were so (Acts 17:11).

Eddie Cloer

An Explanation For the Reader

The beginning of the nineteenth century was characterized by periods of intense spiritual fervor and a great revival of interest in religion in the United States. Thousands attended religious meetings and studied the Bible in a climate of complete freedom of religion and expression.

People in many parts of the country began to question religious practices and creeds. They were troubled by the religious division so prevalent at the time. Some of them began calling for the "restoration" of Christianity to its simplicity of apostolic times. Men from various denominations began to urge others to be simply Christians, without any denominational affiliation.

Two of these men were the father and son Thomas and Alexander Campbell, who came to the U.S. from Scotland. Alexander (1788–1866) became a powerful preacher, writer, and debater. His plea for people to cast aside denominational affiliations and be just Christians was accepted by many. Those who opposed him began to call these Christians "Campbellites" in derision. He replied to this, "I have no idea of adding to the catalogue of new sects. This game has been played too long. I labor to see sectarianism abolished, and all Christians of every name united upon the one foundation on which the apostolic church was founded."[1]

J. N. Armstrong, in these studies, refuted the notion that New Testament Christians could be called "Campbellites," as was charged by some who opposed them in the early twentieth century.

We read in the New Testament that the disciples were called Christians for the first time in Antioch (Acts 11:26). Some believe this name was given to believers in derision by pagans. I do not! The apostle Peter said, "But if a man suffer as a Christian, let him not be ashamed; but let him glorify God in this name" (1 Peter 4:16). What a beautiful way to describe a believer who has been immersed into Christ! "For as many of you as were baptized into Christ did put on Christ" (Galatians 3:27).

Don Shackelford

---

[1]Alexander Campbell, "Reply to 'T. T.,'" *The Christian Baptist* 3 (6 Feb. 1826): 146.

About the Author

John Nelson Armstrong was born January 6, 1870, and died August 12, 1944. He taught in six Christian colleges and was president of four of them. Greek was the joy of his life, and he buried himself in it. Under James A. Harding he read the works of Xenophon, Thucydides, Plato, Homer, and other classical Greek writers. He loved the *Apology* especially, both for the integrity of Socrates and for the grace and beauty of Plato's language. As his knowledge of Greek grew, he called it "the most perfect instrument with which to express thought ever used by mortal tongue, the language that could express the most delicate shades of meaning, the language in which we can almost read the very impulses of the heart of the writer." He believed it was the perfect instrument for God to give men a revelation of Himself.[1]

Armstrong's greatness was not merely in his academic achievements. The documented cases of his sacrifice for Christian education are amazing. R. N. Gardner, president of Western Bible and Literary College in

---

[1] L. C. Sears, *The Biography of John Nelson Armstrong: For Freedom* (Austin, Tex.: Sweet Publishing Co., 1969), 32.

Odessa, Missouri, said of Armstrong, "I know of only a few men who have sacrificed as he has to do good. He looked not on his own things but to the things of others."[2] He served as president of Harding College (now University) from 1924 until 1936. Although some may have forgotten the extent of his work and others have not been informed, Armstrong's influence remains strong on the campus today.

In preparation for accreditation at Cordell Christian College in Cordell, Oklahoma, President Armstrong raised the money to increase the library; and as further help to the library one year, he and three other teachers gave their salaries for the entire year for the purchase of books. During this time they lived on the small incomes from their preaching. George S. Benson, the next president of Harding, said that Armstrong gave his life to Harding, that he carried it through the dark years when he had to go without salary to pay the other teachers.

Armstrong had a clear concept of what a Christian school should be. He wrote, "To guide a mind to think truly and wisely, to judge properly, reason correctly, is masterful work." However, he understood a Christian education to be more than that. He continued,

> . . . in this mind, even in the lowest type of man, is something still more beautiful and wonderful. By some it is called conscience, and by others the moral sense. . . . Call it what we may, it separates man from all other animals and fixes his destiny eternally different. . . . So in our

---

[2]Ibid., 90.

work our chief aim is to send every boy and girl home at night with a tenderer conscience, a greater respect for right and duty. To teach a boy how to live a hundred years and train him to be an intellectual giant without this conscience culture is to curse the world and him.[3]

"We have long been trying to *reform* men," he said. "Only in very recent years have we learned that our real business is *formation* and not *reformation*." His formula for building students into citizens of great character was to ". . . produce the boy with the nobler ideals, with spiritual vision, and with the power to see and to grasp the higher values of life."[4]

In addition to his positive teaching, Armstrong's personality permeated the whole institution. His kindness, generosity, fairness, and faith were contagious. He brought confidence and happiness wherever he went. Both he and Mrs. Armstrong treated the students as their own children. A student whose father had died in the spring was determined to defy the blizzards and shiver the winter through without a coat. Concerned for his health, the Armstrongs provided an overcoat for him. The secret of Armstrong's relationship with students was that he loved them, and they instinctively responded to his love. He was always ready to do anything possible for them. He taught a Greek class one whole year for just one student, G. W. Kieffer.

Armstrong's stirring chapel speeches on "Liberty

---

[3]Ibid., 115.
[4]Ibid., 119.

Is Found in Doing Right" moved students to correct wrongs and established in them a sound basis of moral values. Mrs. Earl Smith said, "We never heard a man speak that equaled him in moving students to want to do right. I remember how my own heart was touched and moved to do what I believed to be right if the whole world turned against me. I could never understand how anyone could ever deviate from the right after being in his classes and hearing his chapel talks." He emphasized in classes and in chapel talks that it is not rules or laws, but principles, that make men: "A girl or boy is not what he is in broad daylight with guards standing around, but what he is in the dark with no one to see him but God. Great men and women have been great because, like Daniel, they had principles they could not violate."

Upon Armstrong's death, God-fearing men and women attempted to evaluate his influence. "If the author of the Hebrew letter were writing today, brother Armstrong would undoubtedly be listed with the great heroes of faith," one said. Another said, "He always prayed as if he had one hand in the hand of God." Still another commented, "His silent influence was far-reaching. To my mind the success of Harding College was due for the most part to J. N. Armstrong."

Armstrong's "silent influence" need not be limited to the name of a dormitory and a few pictures. One who gave so much to Christian education and to the church can still teach and encourage. Please study the lessons presented in this publication. Brother Armstrong would say, as Paul said, "Be ye imitators of me, even as I also am of Christ" (1 Corinthians 11:1).

J. N. Armstrong's study takes the reader to the Bible

and does not permit him to leave it. Other works are cited, and illustrations are given; but again and again, the reader is taken to the original source—the Scriptures. Here is a beautiful picture of undefiled Christianity, painted by a loving, honest, and knowledgeable man.

Burl Curtis

Preface

In offering to the public this little book on "Undenominational Christianity," I have no apology to make. It has seemed to me for years that the Christian world stood in dire need of some direct teaching along this line.

I do not claim to offer in this book a "finished job" in any sense, for the work has been done amid the rush of daily school duties; in fact, the book is made of articles that have appeared in the *Gospel Herald*. It is simply an earnest message sent on its way to honest, God-fearing hearts; a plain scriptural lesson for a plain people. If the unity for which Christ prayed be advanced one step, the desired result shall have been attained.

J. N. Armstrong
1913

UNDENOMINATIONAL CHRISTIANITY— AN INTRODUCTION

The world today practically knows nothing of un‐denominational Christianity. For many, the idea that a person can be only a Christian is hard to accept. As soon as one affirms that he is a Christian, the invariable question is "To what denomination do you belong?" The idea that a person can be a Christian and not belong to some denomination is even denied. Should one dare to claim he is a Christian and deny any denominational affiliation, a denominational name will be thrust upon him.

Suppose a dozen such Christians began to work and worship as a congregation of believers, claiming non-fellowship with any and all denominations. Even if they claimed to be Christians and only Christians, members of the church of Christ and only that, the inevitable would happen: Without investigation, they would be labeled a denomination.

Many think it impossible for Christians to be only Christians and a church to be only a church of Christ. I presume nobody would deny such an honor and distinction to the church which was at Jerusalem in the days when men spoke by the Spirit of God. The first seven chapters of the Book of Acts give the history of the organization and early work of this congregation. It had its thousands of members, yet all of these believers were only Christians. None of them claimed to be more than a disciple of our Lord. Every individual, in being saved, was added by the Lord to the church—which church? To what denomination did all these Christians belong? There was not one on the earth at that time to which they could have belonged.

If thousands of people at Jerusalem became disciples of Christ, were saved, and added to the church—none of them belonging to a denomination, but only to "the church"—why may not thousands of people do and be the same today? Why are we denied the privilege of being just such Christians, disciples, and saved people as they were? If they could be saved, live the Christian life, and work for and worship God simply as disciples and as members of "the church," why may I not do it? What hinders me? If these people were added to "the church," being guided by the very apostles of our Lord, is it not safe, entirely safe, for us to be as they were? In fact, is it not exceedingly dangerous to ignore this holy example of the Spirit in the inspired apostles? "For as many as are led by the Spirit of God, these are the sons of God" (Romans 8:14).[1]

---

[1]Unless otherwise noted, Scripture quotations are taken from the American Standard Version, revised by the American Revision Committee in 1901.

To fail to follow this example of the early disciples is certainly to fail to follow the leadership of the Spirit of God, and to fail to follow the Spirit of God is to fail to be obedient children of God. The only way for us to be faithful children of God is to follow explicitly the Holy Spirit; and to follow the Holy Spirit is to belong to no denomination, but is to be disciples only, Christians only, saved and added to His church because we are saved.

Isn't the religion of our Lord, given to the world through His inspired apostles and prophets, good enough? Isn't it pure enough? Would we dare to offer an improvement on it?

Suppose one takes the New Testament of our Lord, faithfully studies it, and heartily surrenders himself to its Christ, obeying from the heart the commandments of this Lord. If he persistently strives to do and be what this Christ of the New Testament teaches him—and refuses to do or be anything except as Christ leads him—what will he become, and what will he be? He will certainly be a disciple of Christ, will certainly find salvation, and will certainly be added to "the church." In fact, he will be very much like the Jerusalem disciples.

Now suppose a hundred such religionists live in one town. If they come together to worship God as a congregation, knowing no Lord but Jesus and no church save the church to which the Lord added them as they were being saved, what church will these hundred disciples constitute in that town? To what denomination will they belong? None, of course; they will belong simply to the church established by Christ.

2

Undenominational Christianity— Is It Possible?

Many of the teachers of this day teach people to become Christians and then "to join the church of their choice." Thus they are admitting that men become Christians separate and apart from denominational affiliation—that it is possible for one to become a Christian, and only a Christian, without and independent of all denominationalism. Therefore, I do not have to argue or prove that, according to the popular teaching of the age, the first thing to be done on the part of one desiring to become a worshiper of God is to become a Christian.

Neither do I have to prove that, according to this popular teaching, people not only become Christians first, but they are saved by the blood of Jesus, bought, redeemed, and purchased by the price, the precious blood of the Lamb of God, before entering a denomination. These are all admitted facts. No denomination in this country will receive a member into its fellowship until it believes that person to be a Christian, one who has been saved. The various religious groups claim careful work at this point, stressing its importance. Waiving, then, for the present the question of whether or not these teachers tell the people how to become Christians, it is admitted by all that people must be saved, children of God, Christians, before they can be denominationalists. This admitted fact is worthwhile in this discussion; at least, it gives us a start.

To admit that one may hear of Christ, may come to Christ, even to His blood, may be saved, and may have his name enrolled in the Lamb's book of life without even a stain of denominationalism on him is to admit much. It is enough, also, to cause one who wants to please God to wonder why all this denominationalism exists anyhow. Then the question to be discussed is whether this saved man, this child of God, this Christian, has to join a denomination to belong to a church, to have church affiliation, and to be a regular attendant at church.

It will not be doubted that the three thousand souls added to the number of disciples on the Day of Pentecost were saved people, Christians; for it is said, ". . . the Lord added to them day by day those that were [being] saved" (Acts 2:47b). Nor will it be denied that these disciples were "together" and that they "continu[ed] stedfastly with one accord in the temple, . . . praising God" (Acts 2:46, 47a). Neither will it be denied that these people, "together" in the temple "praising God," made up a church, working in a "church capacity," and that all of these disciples belonged to that church. To be sure, we may follow the history of these people and find two of their preachers, Peter and John, imprisoned for preaching in His name; but after consultation, the preachers were permitted to return "to their own company" (Acts

4:23), to which company they reported their experience as prisoners. Then this company "when they heard it, lifted up their voice to God with one accord," and prayed (Acts 4:24); "And when they had prayed, the place was shaken wherein they were gathered together; . . . and they spake the word of God with boldness" (Acts 4:31). Therefore, these people—these saved people—were meeting together and in an assembled capacity were worshiping God, praising Him, and praying to Him. Can we be mistaken in calling such meetings "church meetings"? Could it be a mistake to say that these saved people, thus meeting and worshiping "together," constituted a "church," and that they were actually meeting and worshiping in a "church capacity"? Lest we go too fast and conclude too much, we appeal again to the records. If the Holy Spirit called these people a "church," then we shall be satisfied.

> Now in these days, when the number of the disciples was multiplying, there arose a murmuring of the Grecian Jews against the Hebrews, because their widows were neglected in the daily ministration. And the twelve called the multitude of the disciples unto them, and said, It is not fit that we should forsake the word of God, and serve tables. Look ye out therefore, brethren, from among you seven men of good report, . . . whom we may appoint over this business . . . (Acts 6:1–5).

They selected the men, and the apostles appointed them "over this business." Thus we find these people at Jerusalem meeting again. In this assembled capacity, they were at work, selecting and appointing workers over a certain work. (May I say "church work"?) "And the word of God increased; and the number of the disciples multiplied in Jerusalem exceedingly; and a great company of the priests were obedient to the faith" (Acts 6:7).

The number of the disciples was multiplying in Jerusalem. What was this group that was so actively engaged in religious services—praying, praising, preaching, and saving sinners? Are we ready to call it a church? Shall we say that we have actually found disciples of the Lord, saved people, working and worshiping in a "church capacity" just as disciples of the Lord, and that daily other saved people were being added to them? While we feel that we could in all safety call these people a church, we shall feel all the more safe when we find the Holy Spirit so calling them: "And there arose on that day a great persecution against the church which was in Jerusalem" (Acts 8:1b).

Really, these very people—these very disciples whom we have seen meeting together for prayer and praise, for preaching the gospel and selecting men to see after the poor—were called by the Holy Spirit Himself "the church which was in Jerusalem" (Acts 8:1; 11:22). Surely, that is enough. Every saved person at Jerusalem was a member of a church, yet it cannot be claimed that the church at Jerusalem was a denomination. Indeed, every denomination will admit that this church in Jerusalem, including every saved one in the city, was God's church. Therefore, these disciples—these Christians, these saved people—lived and died simply and only as disciples of Christ, Christians, having never so much as heard of a denomination.

Truly, we have found undenominational Christianity pure and simple, which all the world will acknowledge as pure Christianity. With it, too, we have found God's people of one heart and one soul; there were no divisions among them, but they were being perfected together in the same mind and in the same judgment (1 Corinthians 1:10). This was the holy prayer of our Savior, that all believers might be one (John 17:20, 21). Here it was really answered. With denominationalism, how may divisions ever cease—and how may the prayer of our Master be answered?

UNDENOMINATIONAL CHRISTIANITY— IS IT REQUIRED?

According to the records given us by the Holy Spirit, not one of the disciples brought to Christ on the Day of Pentecost was consulted about "joining the church." Absolutely no "choice of church relation" was given in those days. No preacher ever said to these "new converts," "Join the church of your choice." There was but one church, and all the saved belonged to it—not because they had "joined" it, not because they preferred it to some other church, but because they had been bought with the precious blood of our Lord. The very day, hour, and minute in which they were redeemed by the blood, they were God's by right of purchase. Being His, they were added to His people, the body created by the Lord; for He added daily such as were being saved. These people constituted the saved on earth, the church which was at Jerusalem.

Now, the first Christians were nothing but Christians, religiously speaking. They belonged to no denomination, but were simply undenominational Christians and belonged only to the church of God, the saved. They belonged to this people because God had added them to His church. If they lived and died this way, and only this way, who can deny me the right to become, to live, and to die as these first Christians did? Who can deny that it is my right to be a Christian such as they were and that it is my imperative duty to be so?

Can I be a faithful follower of the Holy Spirit and be more than these Christians were? The first Christians on the earth were free from denominationalism; that is, they belonged to no denomination. If they were so directed by the Holy Spirit, will one not have to depart from the Holy Spirit's leadership to be a denominational Christian? It is my inalienable right and my imperative duty to be a Christian and only a Christian; in no other way can I faithfully follow the Holy Spirit. May I, therefore, be allowed to make a faithful effort to follow the Spirit's instruction without having thrust upon me a denominational name and without being accused of trying to un-Christianize others?

It is my obligation, laid upon me by Heaven, to lead every soul possible to the blood of Christ so that he may be saved. It is my duty to bring every soul under the holy and safe leadership of the Spirit of God. Since Christians made by the divine Spirit were undenominational Christians, does it not become my duty to help and encourage everyone who wants to please God to strive to be such a Christian as the Holy Spirit led people to be in New Testament times? For this reason, I exhort all who want to be Christians—just such Christians as the Holy Spirit led souls to be in earlier days—to strip themselves of denominationalism and to have no fellowship with it. Certainly, no Christian can affiliate with and fellowship denominationalism while following the Holy Spirit, for the divine Spirit never led a Christian into denominationalism. That truth is more certain than that the sun will rise in the morning.

It is not a question, then, of whether the Holy Spirit was the founder of the denominationalism of this age; for it is certain that He was not. Rather, the question is "Am I content to be just such a Christian as those made by His holy instruction?" The question I must ask myself is "Am I satisfied with His plain simplicity, or am I willing to take the responsibility for disregarding His divine pattern?" To be sure, God does not force people to be His servants, but leaves them free to choose. Indeed, some individuals prefer to follow the wisdom of men in religion (the consummation of which wisdom is the denominationalism of this age) rather than the wisdom of our God. God allows this, but He warns,

> Know thou, that for all these things God will bring thee into judgment (Ecclesiastes 11:9c).

> And now, O Israel, hearken unto the statutes and unto the ordinances, which I teach you, to do them; that ye may live, and go in and possess the land which Jehovah, the God of your fathers, giveth you. Ye shall not add unto the word which I command you, neither shall ye diminish from it, that ye may keep the commandments of Jehovah your God which I command you (Deuteronomy 4:1, 2).

What thing soever I command you, that shall ye observe to do: thou shalt not add thereto, nor diminish from it (Deuteronomy 12:32).

Not every one that saith unto me, Lord, Lord, shall enter into the kingdom of heaven; but he that doeth the will of my Father who is in heaven (Matthew 7:21).

Whosoever goeth onward and abideth not in the teaching of Christ, hath not God: he that abideth in the teaching, the same hath both the Father and the Son (2 John 9).

I testify unto every man that heareth the words of the prophecy of this book, If any man shall add unto them, God shall add unto him the plagues which are written in this book: and if any man shall take away from the words of the book of this prophecy, God shall take away his part from the tree of life, and out of the holy city, which are written in this book (Revelation 22:18, 19).

The Holy Spirit, throughout His teaching and in strong terms, forbids all additions, subtractions, amendments, and alterations to His teaching. We know this as certainly as we know that we must die. Denominationalism, with all of its complications and contrivances, is an addition made by human "wisdom" to the simplicity of Christ. That fact is as sure as the fact that Jesus arose from the grave. The Holy Spirit stoutly forbids additions to His work. Through Christ He has given undenominational Christianity only. It is inexplicable, then, how devoted hearts—hearts determined to follow the Spirit of God in religion—can continue in denominational Christianity. What will you do about it? It is your responsibility.

Undenominational Christianity— How Is It Possible?

Just before Jesus left the earth to be exalted at the right hand of the Father as a Prince and a Savior, He said to His disciples, "Tarry ye in the city, until ye be clothed with power from on high" (Luke 24:49b). Even before His death, Jesus had promised them the Holy Spirit, who would guide them into all truth. Again, He "charged them not to depart from Jerusalem, but to wait for the promise of the Father, which, said he, ye heard from me: for John indeed baptized with water; but ye shall be baptized in the Holy Spirit not many days hence" (Acts 1:4, 5).

Soon after giving this charge, Jesus was taken up from them, "and a cloud received him out of their sight" (Acts 1:9b). "Then returned they unto Jerusalem" (Acts 1:12a). We read in Acts 2,

> . . . they were all together in one place. And suddenly there came from heaven a sound as of the rushing of a mighty wind, and it filled all

the house where they were sitting. And there appeared unto them tongues parting asunder, like as of fire; and it sat upon each one of them. And they were all filled with the Holy Spirit, and began to speak with other tongues, as the Spirit gave them utterance (vv. 1–4; read also Acts 1:9–12).

This is a record of the fulfillment of the promise of the Savior that the apostles would be clothed with power from on high. That truth will not be denied by any intelligent Bible student. Our Lord was unwilling for these disciples to go forth to save the world until the Holy Spirit filled them and gave them utterance. We may justly conclude that the work they did after they were thus clothed with power was the work of the Holy Spirit. No one should doubt that He did exactly what He came to do, which was to guide them into all truth. Surely their work as teachers, ever after, was the work of the Holy Spirit. To follow them is certainly to follow the Holy Spirit.

No one can claim the guidance of the Holy Spirit in his religious life if he goes contrary to work done by these apostles who were filled with power from on high. In other words, a religionist is guided by the Holy Spirit just so far as his religious life and practice are in harmony with the life and practice of those who were clothed with the Spirit's power. He who faithfully follows those who were guided by the divine Spirit is free from denominationalism; he belongs to no denomination, but is simply a Christian, a disciple of the Lord. All who thus follow the Guide who directed these teachers are members of the same church to which they belonged, the church of God. Members of God's church today became members in the same way as the people who were guided by this power. That is, they did not "join the church," but God added them to His saved ones as they "were [being] saved." Thus the saved constitute His church. Surely, no one will question that everyone who faithfully follows the Holy Spirit will be saved or that God will be as kind to them as He was to those who followed the Spirit at Jerusalem. If these concepts are accepted as true, then we understand that every such one is saved and, by the Lord, is added to His church.

The reader's fairness and goodness of heart must be trusted not to misunderstand this teaching. It is true that one may be guided by the Holy Spirit unto salvation and be added to the very church of God itself, but then go into denominationalism, "joining" or becoming affiliated with a denomination. One who does so thus becomes a denominational Christian, belonging to two churches; for he was added to the church of our Lord when he was saved but afterwards joined a man-made institution *called* a church. This very thing is sometimes done by noble hearts. However, every step required to become a denominationalist goes beyond the teaching of the Holy Spirit and is contrary to His very earnest pleadings.

Denominationalism is contrary to the example of every Christian and of every church in New Testament history. Not one single Christian in all New Testament times was ever guided by the inspired apostles or prophets to join a denomination. He who becomes more than a Christian—more than a disciple of the Lord and a member of His holy church—takes upon himself the responsibility for going contrary to the instructions and examples of the holy men guided by God's own Spirit.

If one is willing to accept such a responsibility even with God's pleadings against it, that is his business; but my business is to lay the responsibility at his door. I leave it there. It is just as easy for people to be only Christians now as it was in New Testament times; the only reason that people are not is either that they are unwilling to be or that they lack knowledge of the truths about Christ.

Soon after the Holy Spirit came upon the disciples, a large congregation came together. Peter—or rather, the Holy Spirit, using Peter as an instrument—seized the opportunity and began to preach. Jesus had told His disciples to go to Jerusalem and "tarry," or "wait," till the power came upon them. Then they were to preach the gospel to every creature. They had gone, they had waited, and the Holy Spirit had come and entered into them; thus they were prepared to preach.

Peter was an undenominational Christian, or disciple. As an undenominational teacher and preacher, he represented no denomination; he was simply a member of the church to which the Lord adds the saved. Surely, then, his work was undenominational work and could have built up no denomination. His audience was composed of Jews who had come from far and near to worship God, the Lord's own Father. While these were devout Jews, very religious and consecrated in life, they did not believe in Jesus as the Son of God. With this unbelief in their hearts, they had assembled; hence the burden of Peter's preaching was to demonstrate to them that Jesus was the Christ, the Son of God. Fifty days before

UNDENOMINATIONAL CHRISTIANITY—
HOW IS IT POSSIBLE?

this Day of Pentecost, these same Jews had stained their fingers with the very blood of the Son of God, believing that they were putting to death a deceiver. Peter had a fine audience—not a worldly-minded people, not atheists, but men like the Hebrew children and like Daniel, ready to die for God's service. These were prayerful, zealous, and pious people—indeed, a fine audience for this occasion.

First, Peter removed some of their prejudice and mistaken views concerning the wonderful manifestations of power in Jerusalem that morning. He did this by quoting from their Bible, the Old Testament. Then he began his actual sermon:

> Ye men of Israel, hear these words: Jesus of Nazareth, a man approved of God unto you by mighty works and wonders and signs which God did by him in the midst of you, even as ye yourselves know; him, being delivered up by the determinate counsel and foreknowledge of God, ye by the hand of lawless men did crucify and slay: whom God raised up (Acts 2:22–24a).

In this short speech the Holy Spirit, through Peter, preached the life of Jesus. He spoke about His wonders, mighty works, and signs, and about God's approval of His Child. He declared that this audience, using lawless men, had crucified and slain the Son of God and that God had raised Him from the dead. That Jesus had come back from the dead was the proposition to be proved. The Spirit introduced proof, quoting from David, the sweet song writer of Israel in whom these people trusted as a divine teacher and writer. From the quotation, it was certain that David was speaking of someone's resurrection: Either he meant his own, or he was putting the language into another's mouth. The Spirit called attention to the facts that David had died, that he had been buried, and that his tomb remained with them until that day. Therefore, since he could not have meant himself, whom did he mean? The Spirit said that David, being a prophet and knowing that God had sworn to set one of the fruit of David's loins upon his throne, was speaking of the resurrection of the Christ:

> This Jesus did God raise up, whereof we are all witnesses. Being therefore by the right hand of God exalted, and having received of the Father the promise of the Holy Spirit, he hath poured forth this, which ye see and hear. . . . Let all the house of Israel therefore know assuredly, that God hath made him both Lord and Christ, this Jesus whom ye crucified (Acts 2:32–36).

This was enough to strike conviction into the hearts of these honest and devout hearers. By this time, they could almost see blood stains on their hands and feel in their hearts the guilt of having murdered God's own Son. "When they heard this, they were pricked in their heart, and said unto Peter and the rest of the apostles, Brethren, what shall we do?" (Acts 2:37).

Were they convinced? Who would doubt it? Did these crying ones believe Jesus, whom they had crucified fifty days before, to be the Christ, the Son of God?

UNDENOMINATIONAL CHRISTIANITY— HOW IS IT POSSIBLE?

Did they doubt that God had approved Him by His mighty signs? Had they now done what the Spirit had told them to do? That is, did they "know assuredly" that God had made Him both Lord and Christ? If they really did know this great fact of the gospel, and if they knew it as the Spirit in Peter told them to know it—that is, "assuredly," with full confidence, without doubt—then what did they lack to have faith? One is to know without doubt, with full confidence, that Jesus was God's own Child; that His mighty works were God's approval of Him; that He had been crucified, raised from the dead, and exalted at God's right hand as "both Lord and Christ." After one knows all this assuredly, with full confidence, what must he do further in order to believe? Does one who confidently accepts these great facts so his heart is pierced until he cries out, "What shall I do?" need to be told to believe? What more must he believe, and how shall he believe it?

To these believing people—these people who knew assuredly these great truths about Jesus, these convicted people, the Holy Spirit said,

> Repent ye, and be baptized every one of you in the name of Jesus Christ unto the remission of your sins; and ye shall receive the gift of the Holy Spirit. For to you is the promise, and to your children, and to all that are afar off, even as many as the Lord our God shall call unto him (Acts 2:38, 39).

Next, the divine record tells us, "They then that received his word were baptized: and there were added unto them in that day about three thousand souls. . . . And the Lord added to them day by day those that were saved" (Acts 2:41–47b).

Let us remember that we are reviewing a "church meeting" free from denominationalism. We are beholding a church at work, saving the world. The teaching came from the Holy Spirit sent by our Lord, and the man through whom He was speaking was a member of this undenominational church, simply a Christian. All of this teaching was undenominational teaching, pure and simple. At this undenominational church meeting, this undenominational teacher called on unbelievers to "know assuredly," without doubt, that Jesus was "both Lord and Christ." All who did know and were convicted in their hearts were commanded, "Repent ye." Thus, at this undenominational meeting, unsaved people were commanded to accept without doubt the great facts of the gospel, then to repent, and at last to be baptized "in the name of Jesus Christ unto the remission of . . . sins."

By irrefutable logic, then, it follows that he today who preaches Jesus in the way Peter did is teaching undenominational teaching. To do so, he must preach Jesus as the approved Son of God, the resurrected and coronated Lord and Christ. He must call upon the unsaved to believe, or know "assuredly." Then he must exhort all who know these truths to repent and be baptized in the name of Jesus Christ unto the remission of their sins.

Likewise, everyone who is pierced in the heart by knowing "assuredly" that Jesus is Lord and Christ, who repents, and is baptized in the name of Jesus Christ unto the forgiveness of his sins, is saved. He thus becomes a disciple of the Lord, simply a Christian, and is added to the church of our Lord. Church work today that duplicates the Spirit's work which has been recorded for our learning is as approved of God and as Spirit-directed as it was at this undenominational meeting. If this were not so, the Bible would be of no value to us.

5

UNDENOMINATIONAL CHRISTIANITY— WHAT IS IT?

The purpose of this study is to stir every reader to a holy desire to be just such a Christian as Peter, James, John, and Paul were. Such Christians composed the entire church at Jerusalem. No other goal is worthy of the efforts of a Christian, nor is any other pleasing to God. I am persuaded that many people want to please God—that they would rather please Him than do anything else. Indeed, I like to believe that, with their whole hearts, they want to follow the Lord in all that they do. Therefore, if they are denominational Christians, it is because they do not know that denominationalism is displeasing to God. This study is written for such hearts.

Let us not forget that the whole religious world agrees that the first Christians were undenominational Christians. They were members of the church because the Lord added them to it. These Christians held undenominational meetings like the one described in Acts 2. They met in praise and prayer to God, brought unsaved people to these meetings, preached the gospel, saved sinners, appointed servants, cared for the poor—in fact, did all kinds of church work—without affiliation with any denomination. They lived simply as Christians and members of that body of saved people created by the Lord's adding day by day those who were saved. This body of saved ones was called by the Holy Spirit "the church which was in Jerusalem" (Acts 8:1; 11:22).

In the previous chapter, we saw by an examination of the divine records that Jesus promised the Holy Spirit to His disciples to guide them into all truth. He commanded them to wait in Jerusalem until they were clothed with power from heaven. By the eye of faith, we saw them go to Jerusalem and wait for the power. In the same way, we saw the Holy Spirit come, enter into them, and begin His work. As an undenominational Teacher—through an undenominational preacher, Peter—this Spirit from God taught undenominational Christianity, made undenominational Christians, and built up an undenominational church, "the church which was in Jerusalem."

Remember, too, the thoughts at the close of the previous chapter. He who conducts church meetings as this one was conducted, preaches the same truths taught in this meeting, and calls on unsaved people to do the things demanded of the unsaved at this meeting at Jerusalem is likewise conducting undenominational meetings and teaching undenominational Christianity. Further, those who receive such teaching become undenominational Christians. In no other way can we have undenominational Christianity, but by faithfully duplicating this work of the Holy Spirit. This is the "how" of undenominational Christianity: He who faithfully follows the Holy Spirit in His work with these Christians at Jerusalem can be nothing but a Christian.

When the Holy Spirit came with the noise of a hurricane into Jerusalem, it collected a vast crowd together, a congregation of unbelievers in Christ, the very crowd that had crucified Him fifty days before. The first work to be done with this congregation of sinners, crucifiers of the Lord of glory, was to show them that they had really killed the Son of God. Hence the Holy Teacher in Peter began to preach Jesus, affirming Him as both Lord and Christ, exalted at the right hand of God. After Peter had, with irrefutable facts, proved Jesus to be the Son of God, he called upon the unbelievers to "know assuredly, that God hath made him both Lord and Christ, this Jesus whom ye crucified" (Acts 2:36). This irrefutable testimony of Peter, guided by the Holy Spirit, sent conviction to their hearts. With heart-distressing agony, they cried out for relief of heart and soul.

Again, we halt to view the work. What was really done, and how was it accomplished? Certainly, we have seen nothing done in this meeting thus far but powerful preaching. The preacher has labored hard to establish in every heart the great truth that Jesus was all He claimed to be; that they, with wicked hands, had murdered Him; and that God had raised Him from the grave and exalted Him at His own right hand both Lord and Christ. With great and convincing argument, he hurled this truth home to thousands of hearts until they burst with distress. All this effect was accomplished by preaching Jesus to them. No other effort was made.

When these people came together to hear this sermon, they believed that Jesus' body was sleeping in the earth, that all His claims had been false, and that they had been right fifty days before in nailing Him to the cross. They believed that they had done service to God. How changed were these honest hearts! How grieved they were! After hearing Peter speak, they believed the very opposite—namely, that all of Jesus' claims had been true, that they actually had slain the Christ of God, and that He was alive again, Lord and Christ at God's right hand. This must have been their faith, and it was this conviction that distressed them.

Aware of all this faith, conviction, and grief of heart among his listeners, the preacher helped their distressed hearts. To relieve them, he said, "Repent ye." Therefore, the change wrought in these hearts that caused them to cry out—the grief and sorrow in them—did not include repentance. All the change thus far, even the cry itself, was outside and independent of repentance. The change in them, then, is a change to be wrought in unsaved hearts before repentance. This is as certain as the fact that the Holy Spirit replied to their cry of grief. In order to relieve them of this grief and sorrow, they were told to repent. May we never forget that this is undenominational teaching!

What was this great something that caused the effects of grief and sorrow? Certainly, a great change had come into these hearts. This change caused grief and sorrow, but it came before repentance. Surely, it was faith in Jesus as the Lord and Christ. This much faith, then, must certainly precede repentance and does precede repentance in every conversion to Christ. To be undenominational in my teaching, I must teach that this change comes before repentance.

UNDENOMINATIONAL CHRISTIANITY—
WHAT IS IT?

Indeed, the Holy Spirit in Paul taught this same order. "I now rejoice, not that ye were made sorry, but that ye were made sorry unto repentance; for ye were made sorry after a godly sort, that ye might suffer loss by us in nothing. For godly sorrow worketh repentance unto salvation" (2 Corinthians 7:9, 10a).

Without doubt, the members of this crowd we are considering had sorrow—in fact, godly sorrow. To them Peter said, "Repent ye." This was Heaven's order.

I would like to sit down with each reader and have a "heart-to-heart" talk about these matters. It is essential to the salvation of the world that the saints of the Lord be as these early Christians were—that is, "of one heart and soul" (Acts 4:32). There are to be no divisions among us. We are to be perfectly joined together in the same mind and in the same judgment, "that the world may believe that thou hast sent me" (John 17:21c).

I am trying to be fair in the examination of this undenominational meeting of Christ's people. Really, the Spirit has been so plain in His record of the meeting that I cannot see a place for honest hearts to disagree. If we are glad to be like these early disciples and to do as they did, then I do not believe that we can disagree about these inspired facts.

Of course, if one among us has a teaching of his own, or of some other man, and we love this theory more than we love the union of saints and the truth of our Lord, then we can assuredly find something in the divine record to support our theory. If one is affiliated with a denomination and is determined to continue in this affiliation, then simple, undenominational teaching will not change him. I earnestly entreat all honest seekers of truth to let the plain facts of this meeting directed by the Holy Spirit weigh heavily upon their hearts. Please share the Wise Man's view of following God's words:

> Let them not depart from thine eyes; keep them in the midst of thy heart. For they are life unto those that find them. . . . Keep thy heart with all diligence; for out of it are the issues of life. . . . And let thine eyelids look straight before thee. Make level the path of thy feet, and let all thy ways be established. Turn not to the right hand nor to the left: remove thy foot from evil (Proverbs 4:21–27).

Again, let us move forward in our examination of this meeting at Jerusalem. These grieved and sorrowing hearts were told, "Repent ye, and be baptized every one of you in the name of Jesus Christ unto the remission of your sins . . ." (Acts 2:38). Remember that this answer was given to distressed hearts to relieve them of the weight of the awful sin of murdering the Son of God. This was the sin that weighed heavily on their hearts. They were in deep sorrow for having done it and were ready, heartily ready, to fix it—but how could it be fixed? "What shall we do?" was the cry of their hearts (Acts 2:37b). They surely wondered whether or not anything could be done to rid them of so terrible a sin. The answer was "Repent." Peter was saying, in effect, "Surrender yourselves to Christ the Lord. Make His will yours. Unreservedly turn yourself unto Him." He told the people, "Be baptized every one of you in the name of Jesus Christ unto the remission of your sins; and ye shall receive the gift of the Holy Spirit" (Acts 2:38).

All of us are heartily agreed that the Holy Spirit, in giving this answer, was including the conditions of pardon, or riddance of guilt, for these hearts. Somewhere in complying with the terms of this answer, they would find relief, riddance of guilt, and pardon. We may be certain that this riddance did not come until after repentance. When they repented, giving themselves unreservedly to Christ, they were told to be baptized for the forgiveness of their sins. This is the only time that riddance or pardon from sin is mentioned in the entire record (though it was the very thing burdening the hearts of the inquirers). This one time, the distressed hearts were told to be baptized "unto the remission" of their sins. Is it possible that these hearts had already reached, or come unto, the very thing that they were here told to be baptized unto? Of course not. Further, these hearts were promised the gift of the Holy Spirit after their baptism.

The record says, "They then that received his word were baptized: and there were added unto them in that day about three thousand souls" (Acts 2:41). In those days God was adding to the saved "those that were [being] saved" (Acts 2:47). We have seen that these people constituted the church of God and that they were members because, and when, they were added—and not until then. These three thousand souls were added after baptism and became members of God's church when they were added to it.

The Scriptures are clear that in this undenominational meeting, people were told to believe ("know assuredly"), to repent, and to be baptized unto the forgiveness of sins. It is also scripturally certain that people were added to the saved body of disciples after being baptized and that they were given the gift of the Holy Spirit after their baptism. These are significant facts that the honest heart will weigh.

We will waive until another time the meaning of "unto" in the expression "unto the remission of . . . sins." However, this much we have already determined: He who teaches people to believe what was taught at this undenominational meeting can read his teaching in the very words of the Bible; he can be certain that he is undenominational and that he is building up the very church of God. What, then, does he teach? He teaches people to believe that Jesus is both Lord and Christ, and he teaches them to believe this unto godly sorrow. He calls upon those believing and consequently sorrowing ones to repent; and he calls upon those believing, sorrowing, and repenting ones to be baptized unto the remission of their sins. He gives them God's promise that they will receive the gift of the Holy Spirit and be added to the saved, the church of God, when they obey. Such a teacher is just the kind of Christian and preacher that Peter was, and those brought to Christ under his preaching are just the kind of Christians as the three thousand. They are members only of the church to which God added them.

Undenominational Christianity— The Only Basis of Union

The Holy Spirit, in His teaching in the New Testament, requires the people of God to be of one heart and one soul. He who does not know that divisions among believers in Christ are sinful and destructive to real Christianity has overlooked the plainest of Bible teaching. "Behold, how good and how pleasant it is for brethren to dwell together in unity!" (Psalm 133:1).

Jesus prayed to His Father,

> Neither for these only do I pray, but for them also that believe on me through their word; that they may all be one; even as thou, Father, art in me, and I in thee, that they also may be in us: that the world may believe that thou didst send me. And the glory which thou hast given me I have given unto them; that they may be one, even as we are one; I in them, and thou in me, that they may be perfected into one; that

the world may know that thou didst send me ... (John 17:20–23).

This prayer of the Savior for every believer in the world to be one with every other believer, as the Father and Son are one, should be enough to convert all true lovers of Christ to the doctrine of the oneness of Christ's people. That Jesus prayed for this very thing in the hour of His deepest concern should make it important to every disciple; indeed, it should place this interest heavily upon each heart. Especially is this so when one knows the Master's purpose for wanting this unity: Possibly no other sin among believers so hinders the world from faith in Christ as does this grievous sin of division.

Paul wrote, "Now I beseech you, brethren, through the name of our Lord Jesus Christ, . . . that ye be perfected together in the same mind and in the same judgment" (1 Corinthians 1:10). With such entreaties on the part of the Holy Spirit for unity, how can a true spirit, an obedient heart, treat lightly this sin among us? How can one fail to feel it imperative upon him to give up anything and everything not specifically required by the Holy Spirit in order to be one with every other disciple? Indeed, one should feel sinfully guilty as long as he is holding to any practice in religion that perpetuates the divisions among Christians.

Two real causes perpetuate divisions in the religious world. One is that many people—some good pious people too—have never regarded it a sin, but treat it lightly and are not concerned about it. The other cause is that many with pious and otherwise faithful hearts, who deeply regret the awful division that exists, consider the trouble too deep-seated ever to be remedied. Neither group makes any effort to bring about the very thing our Lord teaches and commands; rather, each continues in disobedience to God.

Some, however, are ready to "[tread] the winepress alone" (Isaiah 63:3) to obey Jesus. Like Saul of Tarsus, they are crying out in their hearts, "What shall I do, Lord?" (Acts 22:10). They are willing to give up business or social standing and become a "gazing stock," "the filth of the world, the offscouring of all things" (1 Corinthians 4:13b), that they may please their Lord and do His will. For these, I write.

The beautiful result of unity among saints can never be reached so long as denominationalism is perpetuated. He who encourages it is encouraging the very thing that hinders efforts to accomplish the glorious end for which Jesus prayed. Such a one is encouraging the greatest evil in the religious world. Think of it: Some of the best people (in heart) in the world are winking at, encouraging, even supporting that which hinders Christ's cause in the world as few other things have ever done.

We could wish that whole denominational churches would "break line" and "come out of her" (see Revelation 18:4), but we could not realistically hope for it. The only way to stop denominationalism in its onward progress is for individual hearts to see its evils. They must then forsake it, renounce it, and become just such Christians as New Testament Christians were. To be just such Christians as the first Christians were means to be guided absolutely by the Holy Spirit—to teach, work, serve, and worship as He led people to do when He came into the world to guide them into all truth. If we duplicate His work with mankind, we may be certain that we are such Christians as New Testament Christians were, absolutely free of denominationalism.

Jesus would not let the first Christians begin the great work of saving the world until the Holy Spirit came to guide them. The command was to "wait," to "tarry." They did. He came, and we have been examining His first work in and with those disciples. Was Jesus any more anxious to have His first disciples guided by the Holy Spirit than He is to have His disciples today guided by that same Holy Spirit? If He would not let them proceed in their work without the Spirit's guidance, is He willing for us to go on without the same guidance? Anyone today who trustfully and from the heart follows explicitly the work the Spirit did when He came to guide the early disciples is certainly following the Holy Spirit's guidance. In fact, as far as we know, that is the only way to be guided by Him.

As His work with them is to be our example and our guide, and as our work must be true to this divine model, we must examine conscientiously and carefully every phase of the work. We have seen that this first work included preaching about Jesus, hearing, knowing assuredly, repenting, and then being baptized. He, then, who follows this pattern is following the guidance of the Holy Spirit as Peter and his hearers did on the first Pentecost after the resurrection of Jesus. Such a preacher preaches Jesus as He is revealed in the New Testament, entreats his hearers to know confidently that the Jesus who was crucified is Lord and Christ, and commands all who do know it to repent and be baptized for the forgiveness of their sins. He does not preach the doctrines of the various denominations, but Bible doctrine. To label such a preacher with any denominational title is to misrepresent the man himself and the doctrine of our Lord.

With this plain example of the Holy Spirit, how can true hearts be divided in the work of preaching the gospel and saving the world? Is the example plain? Can we follow it? Surely, it is as plain as a well traveled road. No prophet, priest, or preacher is necessary to interpret it so that the unlearned and unschooled may understand it; it is so plain that anyone who reads may comprehend. Is it possible that the Holy Spirit has spoken so confusingly that hearts searching for truth, even for the blood of Jesus, misunderstand? Is the Spirit's teaching so vague that they must separate into parties, each building up his own party, when Jesus begs and entreats them to be of the same mind and the same judgment? Where is the fault? If the Holy Spirit has taught so that hearts cannot understand Him, then the entreaties of the Holy Spirit for us to be one are surely in vain.

Were the people to whom Peter preached saved before or after baptism? Here is a fork in the road. Here good and true hearts separate from one another. Is it necessary? Did the three thousand who were baptized on that Pentecost disagree at this point, or were they one? When the meeting was over, was there one party who believed they were saved before baptism, and another division who believed they were saved after baptism? No, there was not, and everybody knows there was no such division. Why not? Didn't those people assemble from all parts of the world? Didn't they speak different languages, and hadn't they been brought up under different influences and in different environments? In other words, weren't they as varied in their temperaments, dispositions, home influences, and early training as any audience today? Nevertheless, as soon as Peter said, "Be baptized . . . unto the remission of your sins" (Acts 2:38), every one in that vast audience understood Peter's speech. Why can't we? What makes the difference? True, we have a translation of Peter's speech, but is our translation true? Are the English words into which Peter's ideas have been put harder to understand?

In other words, my beloved friends, do you believe that honest hearts ought to misunderstand the little word "unto" in the expression "unto the remission of your sins" so as to separate into parties, building up factions and divisions among God's people while all the time Jesus is praying and entreating that they may be one? Surely, the little word "unto" is not that ambiguous. The meaning of that simple Anglo-Saxon word tells the story. It is the key to the meaning of the passage. "Surely," one may say, "the great division in the religious world on the question of when we are saved—whether before baptism or after—is not over the meaning of words like 'unto.'" Most assuredly, that is the fact! In truth, there is no excuse for the division. Denominationalism can continue only if we completely ignore our Savior's pleadings for us to be one.

When Peter said for these people to be baptized unto the forgiveness of sins, he connected baptism with forgiveness of sins in an important sense. What did he mean? We shall see in the next chapter.

UNDENOMINATIONAL CHRISTIANITY— MAKES DIVISION IMPOSSIBLE

Jesus our Lord gave to the world Christianity, entirely free from denominationalism. That fact is admitted by all fair-minded students of the Bible. As long as Christians were faithful to the guidance of the Holy Spirit, they were free from the curse of denominationalism, being "of one heart and soul" (Acts 4:32).

For that time, every Christian in the world was one with every other Christian, and division was impossible. They all spoke the same truths and were joined together in the same mind and in the same judgment. Husbands and wives, neighbors and friends could sit down and discuss with perfect freedom and pleasantness any and every phase of the teaching of our Lord. They could meet and worship God at the common altar of our Father. All of God's children could meet around the Lord's table and symbolically partake of their Lord's body and drink the representation of His blood. Children did not have to decide on the sad question "Will we join Mother's church or Father's?" There was but one church; father's and mother's influences were one united force in the home to lead the children to be Christians only. No one ever said "Mother's church" or "Father's church"; for there was but one church in the world, and that was the church of God. Every Christian in the world belonged to it. No one ever said, "I will go with you to your church this morning if you will go with me to mine tonight." No husband ever went with his wife to her church and then went on to his. Such talk and such procedures were absolutely impossible, for the simple reason that the holy disciples were one, with no divisions among them. What a happy condition! Who could not wish for such beautiful harmony again?

Especially, we should wish for unity since it is our God's will for it to reign in His saints and since our blessed Lord prayed so earnestly for this oneness. Can a faithful Christian treat lightly so good a thing, a thing so zealously prayed for on the part of the Master, and so plainly required of all saints? However much we may desire this divinely ordained arrangement and condition, it can never be, as long as denominational churches exist. The basic question is this: "Do we prefer denominational churches to our Lord's church?" Would we rather have what we do have than to have that divine and heaven-born child, Christianity, just as it appeared in the earth in its newborn state?

I am persuaded that many hearts are reaching for the genuine article and will accept it; yet how may *all* the disciples, *all* Christians, be one as the Savior prayed? We can accomplish this only by duplicating the work given in the divine records. We must make this work our model. Jesus would not allow this work to be done

UNDENOMINATIONAL CHRISTIANITY—MAKES DIVISION IMPOSSIBLE

until those doing it were being guided by power from on high. It was too important to be left in the hands of mere humans, unaided by the divine Spirit. Therefore, His command was to "wait," to "tarry," until the power came. The disciples could have established a work without this aid from on high, just as we could establish our own work. In fact, they could do even better at this task than we could today, because they had been to school under our Savior for more than three years. If anyone could have proceeded with this great work unaided, they could have. However, the Lord would not allow these men, specially trained by Himself, to go without an infallible Guide. How much more important it is that we today be guided by the same infallible Guide! Hence His work has been written for our guidance. We are urged not to add to it or to take from it, that we may be as perfectly guided as they were. Religious or church work today that is not in harmony with the work done by the Holy Spirit in the apostles of the New Testament is not done under the guidance of the Holy Spirit. In contrast, the work done today in harmony with the records of the New Testament is infallibly guided by the Spirit of God and is therefore undenominational. As this is the only way to be infallibly guided by the Holy Spirit today, I wish to emphasize again the importance of scrutinizing the meeting at Jerusalem so that we may thoroughly understand the divine work, our pattern.

Let no one tire, then, as we again review the records. Some soul may depend on this review for everlasting life. The believing, convicted, and distressed hearts at Jerusalem were commanded by the Spirit to repent and be baptized in the name of Jesus Christ unto the remission, or forgiveness, of their sins. This is the order of the procedure of the work of the Holy Spirit; that is certain. We cannot disagree about these facts and the order of them. We must also agree that, somewhere in the process, these anxious hearts found comfort in the forgiveness of their sins. In other words, they first knew assuredly that God had made Jesus Lord and Christ, then were told to repent, and then were baptized for forgiveness of sins; and somewhere in this obedience, they were forgiven.

According to the King James translation of the Spirit's teaching, Peter said, "Be baptized every one of you in the name of Jesus Christ for the remission of sins" (Acts 2:38). The question is, Were they saved before baptism or after it? All depends on the meaning of the little word "for." If this word "for" means what it does in the sentence "Son, go to town for the mail," then certainly they were not saved before baptism, but were commanded to be baptized to obtain remission of sins. If we are to examine every possibility, we must consider whether or not "for" in Peter's speech could mean what it does in these sentences:

> For this cause shall a man leave his father and mother, and shall cleave to his wife; and the two shall become one flesh (Ephesians 5:31).

> Be subject to every ordinance of man for the Lord's sake (1 Peter 2:13a).

> Blessed are they that have been persecuted for righteousness' sake (Matthew 5:10a).

If this was Peter's meaning in using the word "for," then the three thousand who responded obediently to the Holy Spirit's teaching on the Day of Pentecost were saved before baptism. In other words, the English preposition "for" sometimes means "to obtain," but at other times it means "on account of" or "because of." Every fair student is ready to admit facts; he never loses anything by doing it, but always gains. Which "for" did Peter use? What did Peter mean by the word he used that was translated "for" in the King James Version?

Peter spoke in Greek, and the little word translated "for" in the version mentioned is *eis*. Now, if this little word has the two meanings of "for" in it—namely, one looking forward and the other looking backward—then "for" might be a good translation of the Greek word. However, if it turns out that the Greek word has only one of the meanings of "for," then it is not a good translation, but seems calculated to mislead. On investigation, it is found that the retrospective meaning of the English "for" is never found in the Greek word; it never looks backward. In other words, *eis* never means "on account of" or "because of." No Greek ever used the word Peter used with a retrospective meaning.

When two committees, American and English, began the work that resulted in the Standard Revised Version,[1] a covenant was formed. They determined that they would not change the King James translation except where the original, the Greek, forced a change; and then a change would be made only when two-thirds of the committee said that the original translation required

---

[1]*Note:* This is the American Standard Version.

a change. Under this agreement, they did their work. When they came to the "for" in Acts 2:38, they changed it to "unto." Instead of making Peter say, "Be baptized for" remission of sins, they made him say, "Be baptized unto" remission. In so doing, they translated out of the word "for" the possible meaning "because of" or "on account of." They had to do this in order to make a true translation: The English word "unto" never looks back, but always forward, as does the Greek word used by Peter.

Peter's word, or rather the Holy Spirit's word, *eis*, always follows an expression that indicates or implies motion, and this motion brings the thing involved "to," "unto," or "into" the thing or state indicated by the object controlled by the *eis*. Since it is true that Peter's word never means "because of," or "on account of," but always looks forward, it irrefutably follows that those baptized on the Day of Pentecost came unto, or into, remission of their sins when they were baptized—and not before. It would have been impossible to baptize them "unto" forgiveness if they had come into possession of remission before baptism.

UNDENOMINATIONAL CHRISTIANITY— SAVED AFTER BAPTISM

U.S. President Theodore Roosevelt was a great teacher and leader, respected as a lecturer, a colonel, and a writer. In his line of work, he was almost peerless. Few men have had so many American people sitting at their feet for instruction as did he. They were his disciples—his learners—but not his disciples only. Not many of them would have been so very foolish as to exclude all other teachers and hold to Roosevelt only.

Few of us would encourage another to commit himself so unreservedly to any leader. However, if one made up his mind to be a student only of Roosevelt in politics, believing, teaching, and living doctrines just because Roosevelt taught them, we would not fail to see the faith and loyalty of this heart to that former President. Neither would we fail to see the crown of honor it would place upon that brow.

To show such faith in, demonstrate such loyalty to, and bestow such honor upon a mere man would be more than foolish to free-thinking individuals. In contrast, to prostrate ourselves in that way at the feet of the Man of Galilee is the divine requirement. To be His disciple, and only His disciple, in religion is what Heaven requires:

> No man can serve two masters: for either he will hate the one, and love the other; or else he will hold to one, and despise the other (Matthew 6:24a).

> For one is your teacher, and all ye are brethren (Matthew 23:8b).

> For one is your master, even the Christ (Matthew 23:10b).

> If ye abide in my word, then are ye truly [really] my disciples; and ye shall know the truth, and the truth shall make you free (John 8:31b, 32).

> Whosoever goeth onward and abideth not in the teaching of Christ, hath not God: he that abideth in the teaching, the same hath both the Father and the Son (2 John 9).

He who takes Jesus to be his Teacher—believing, teaching, and living only that endorsed by Christ and sanctifying himself to such a life for the Lord's sake—is truly a follower of Jesus, a disciple of Christ, and only a disciple of Him. If there are Christians on the earth, then without dispute, such a person is one. He is simply and only a Christian. He disclaims any relations, religious or church, save relations to Christ. He stoutly refuses and rejects from his religion all doctrines but Christ's. He refuses to be known save by any name except to be designated as a follower of the Lord.

However far such a one may fall short of his claims, every Bible student must grant that his religious position is thoroughly scriptural. We should be fair enough, too, to admit that this is the position to which every heart that desires to please God must come. Until we are willing to come to this undenominational position, we cannot even hope for the union for which Jesus prayed.

He who does not desire and work for that for which Jesus prayed and worked is unchristian. This is Jesus' test: "If ye were Abraham's children, ye would do the works of Abraham" (John 8:39b). Likewise, we may say, "If you are Christ's, you want what Christ wants, you desire that for which He prayed, and you are working for that toward which Christ works." I am not being unkind when I say that men who encourage denominationalism are encouraging divisions among those professing Christianity. Anyone who encourages divisions does so over the blood-sealed protest of Jesus Christ our Lord and is, therefore, unchristian.

Again, I ask my readers to return with me to that undenominational meeting at Jerusalem. It is important. We want to "see" things alike, if we are truly Christian in heart. Husbands and wives, true ones, want to agree with each other. A beautiful home life is due to the unison of hearts. When husbands and wives do not make an effort to "see" alike, to minimize their differences and magnify their agreements, their home life is wrecked. The Holy Spirit lovingly pleads with God's children to endeavor to keep the unity of the spirit in the bond of peace (Ephesians 4:3). I am certain that this undenominational work at Jerusalem is plain and that there is absolutely no reason for disagreement between loving, loyal hearts.

Several times in the King James Version of the Scriptures, we find the expression "for the remission of sins." It is said that John the Baptist "preach[ed] the baptism of repentance for the remission of sins" (Mark 1:4b; see Luke 3:3). Again, on the Day of Pentecost, as we have seen, Peter said to believing, penitent hearts, "Be baptized every one of you in the name of Jesus Christ for the remission of sins" (Acts 2:38b). Then our Master said when He gave the Lord's Supper, "Drink ye all of it; for this is my blood of the new testament, which is shed for many for the remission of sins" (Matthew 26:27b, 28).

Again, let us examine the meaning of this phrase. It tells the story. Distressed hearts cried out because they were burdened with sin, and especially with the sin of murdering our Lord. They wanted relief, and their wants burst into cries for this relief. All of us agree that they found relief, but honest hearts have disagreed as to when they found it, whether before or after baptism.

As we saw in the previous chapter, the English word "for" is an equivocal, or ambiguous, term with more than one meaning. Lovers of denominational interests have taken advantage of this fact and misled honest hearts, making them believe that "for" in the phrase "for the remission of sins" means "because of" or "on account of." In this way, Peter's speech to those distressed hearts has been made to support the theory that men are saved before baptism.

On investigation, the word "for" in the places cited is found to be translated from the same word in the Greek. Certainly, when Jesus shed His blood for the remission of sins, it was not "because of" remission, but that sins might be remitted. There are no dissenting voices regarding this interpretation. Here we speak the same things and are perfectly joined together in the same mind and in the same judgment. Why is it that we are a unit as to the meaning of "for" in one passage yet disagree as to the meaning of "for" in the other passages, when all three "for's" come from the same Greek word? To be sure, if the word from which these "for's" come had the two meanings that our "for" has, then it might mean "because of" in Peter's speech and "in order to obtain" in Christ's speech. Then the ambiguity might have to be cleared up from other passages. As a matter of fact, there is no such ambiguity in the Holy Spirit's word. The accumulated scholarship of the ages gives the word from which these "for's" came one unequivocal meaning, namely, "looking unto, reaching to (or into) an object, end, or condition." Absolutely, there is not one voice against this prospective meaning of *eis*. This meaning is inherent in the word.

The revised versions—the English Revised Version (1881–85), the American Revised Version, and the Standard American Revised Version (1901) of the King James translation, the work of the ripest scholarship of the world—use a forward-looking word. Scholarly committees were forced by their knowledge of the unquestioned meaning of *eis* to change these "for's" to a word that looks forward; they would have been unfaithful—traitors to a most sacred trust—if they had not done so.

What have they given us? The unequivocal word "unto" has taken the place of "for" in the passages. Hence we have John baptizing "unto remission," Jesus shedding His blood "unto remission," and Peter commanding souls to be baptized "unto remission." The combined scholarship of Europe and America has declared that the word means the same in all of these passages.

W. W. Goodwin, author of *Goodwin's Greek Grammar*, which has been used in the leading colleges and universities of the land, said, "I think *eis* in Acts 2:38 expresses *purpose* or *tendency* and is rightly translated *for* or *unto* (in the sense of *for*)."[1] J. H. Thayer, author of a respected New Testament Greek-English lexicon, said, "I accept the rendering of the revised version 'unto the remission of your sins' (the *eis* expressing the end aimed at and secured by 'repentance and baptism' just previously enjoined)."[2]

James W. Willmarth, a member of the Board of the American Baptist Publication Society, wrote,

> It is feared that if we give to *eis* its natural and obvious meaning, undue importance will be ascribed to Baptism, the Atonement will be undervalued, and the work of the Holy Spirit disparaged. Especially is it asserted that here is the vital issue between Baptists and Camp-

---

[1] W. W. Goodwin, to J. W. Shepherd, 27 July 1893, quoted in J. W. Shepherd, *Handbook on Baptism* (Nashville: Gospel Advocate Co., 1950), 348.
[2] J. H. Thayer, to J. W. Shepherd, 5 May 1893, quoted in Shepherd, 356.

bellites.[3] We are gravely told that if we render *eis* in Acts 2:38 *in order to*, we give up the battle, and must forthwith become Campbellites; whereas if we translate it *on account of*, or *in token of*, it will yet be possible for us to remain Baptists.

. . . It is our business, simply and honestly, to ascertain the exact meaning of the inspired originals. . . . Away with the question—"What *ought* Peter to have said in the interest of orthodoxy?" The real question is, "What *did* Peter say, and what did he *mean*. . . ?". . .

The truth will suffer nothing by giving to *eis* its true signification. When Campbellites translate *in order to* in Acts 2:38 they translate correctly. Is a translation false because Campbellites endorse it?[4]

I could quote from many other scholars who have supported this translation, but these three quotations from *Shepherd's Handbook on Baptism* are sufficient to establish the fact that Peter taught believing, penitent hearts to be baptized so that they might be saved, or receive remission of sins. I am glad, too, as Mr. Willmarth said, that I do not have to avoid this passage, rejecting its obvious meaning. . . . Clearly, the people at the un-

---

[3]"Campbellites" is a term used by Mr. Willmarth, a Baptist, for some who practice undenominational Christianity. He shared their views on baptism.

[4]James W. Willmarth, "Baptism and Remission," *Baptist Quarterly* (July 1877): 304–5; quoted in Shepherd, 357–59.

denominational meeting in Acts 2 were commanded to be baptized so that their sins might be blotted out.

Undenominational Christianity— Remission of Sins

Some good true hearts have failed to accept the plain teaching of the Spirit on baptism because they feared that it gave too much importance to baptism and consequently undervalued the power of Christ's blood.

We, as human beings, are not in a position to pass judgment on the consequences or results of the unequivocal teaching of God. Nevertheless, we may be sure that allowing the Spirit's teaching on baptism to have its natural and obvious meaning in no way detracts from the cleansing power of the blood. All obedience can be acceptable—in fact, can be obedience at all—only as the one rendering it believes in the blood. "Through faith, in his blood" (Romans 3:25), leaning upon and looking to the cleansing power of the blood of the Lamb, one may obey God—and only in this way may one truly obey. No obedience, in and of itself, saves.

Faith itself is just as powerless to save as baptism. Either, without the blood, is but a vain attempt for a blessing. Faith itself is made powerful only by the glorious but shameful death of our Lord.

It took the death of Christ to make it possible for God to save sinners. As God cannot lie, even so He cannot be unjust. Hence God set forth Christ "to be a propitiation, . . . that he might himself be just, and the justifier of him that hath faith in Jesus" (Romans 3:25, 26). In fact, when God permitted Jesus to die on the cross, He was opening the door of mercy, a door He could not otherwise open. He had lovingkindness toward thousands, and His boundless heart was full of mercy; but He could not extend it to sinners and at the same time be just. The death of Jesus, then, makes it possible for God to save sinners at all. Absolutely no conceivable conditions could avail sinners of salvation apart from this blood. Without Christ's blood, one could believe with all the implicitness possible to a human heart, and still the Almighty One could not save him. Otherwise, God was extravagant in the use of His own Child's lifeblood, when that Child was begging the Father with all the intensity of His soul not to use that blood, if it could be helped. No, no, my beloved, God has not put Himself to more cost than was absolutely essential to enable Him to save sinners.

Still, we are not undervaluing the severe expense to which God put Himself when we teach people that faith saves, that without repentance they will perish. Did Paul undervalue the triumphant death of our Lord when he said in Romans 10:9, ". . . if thou shalt confess with thy mouth Jesus as Lord, and shalt believe in thy heart that God raised him from the dead, thou shalt be saved"? Not one of those who fear that the plain teaching concerning baptism detracts from the meritorious death of

Jesus has ever run from this teaching by Paul. Confessing Jesus as Lord was made a condition of salvation by the apostle. How, in the name of all that is good and true, could salvation come from confessing with one's mouth the Lord Jesus Christ? Absolutely nothing in the act itself can save. If it could, then confessing twice or three times should help even more.

Consider this illustration. The cultivation of a crop is a condition on which the crop depends; it causes the crop to grow, and a little cultivation makes a little crop. More cultivation causes more growth. The more thoroughly, or more scientifically, one cultivates the crop, the better the crop will be. Cultivating the crop helps it directly. Confessing Jesus as Lord helps to save the sinner, but *not* as the cultivation helps the crop. How does it help unto salvation? Confessing can help absolutely only as it borrows power from the blood; in other words, it helps to connect the soul, or bring it into contact, with the blood.

Therefore, when Peter said, "Which also after a true likeness doth now save you, even baptism, not the putting away of the filth of the flesh, but the interrogation of a good conscience toward God, through the resurrection of Jesus Christ" (1 Peter 3:21), he was not undervaluing the blood of his Lord. Rather, he was exalting its power to save. To declare that faith, repentance, confession, and baptism—which have no power, no virtue, to save—are given saving power through their connection with the blood is to ascribe power to the blood. These simple acts become obedience to God, being efficacious simply, solely, and only because they are bloodstained. That blood is not the blood of a goat, either, but the blood of our Lord. Certainly, ascribing such power does not undervalue the blood of Christ. Let us not fear or avoid any plain teaching that concerns an act of obedience that derives all of its virtue from the blood.

God has sanctified the simple acts of believing, repenting, and confessing by the blood. He has made these acts efficacious through the blood, when not one of them could avail apart from the blood. If He has actually done this without in any way detracting from the saving power of our Lord's blood, could He not have done as much with the simple act of burying the body in water as an expression of the faith in one's heart? If He could attach importance to believing, repenting, and confessing without minimizing the saving power of the blood, then He could do the same thing concerning baptism. Only those who know His will can truly understand.

Away with our opinions and preconceived notions! Away with our party spirit and ideas of what the Spirit should have said according to the interest of a particular party. They have nothing to do with truth. Let us simply ask, What has God said and what does He mean?

In the previous chapter, we considered comments from three eminent scholars on the meaning of Peter's speech on Pentecost. All three of these scholars agreed that Peter was teaching that repentance and baptism were in order to receive remission of sins and that God, by His Holy Spirit in Peter, actually did teach people to be baptized in order to receive the remission of their sins. No scholar, I presume, would deny that this is the most natural and obvious meaning of Peter's language. As far as I can tell, only those who have a theory to care for, or a party to support, would deny this obvious meaning.

The eminent Baptist scholar James W. Willmarth, from whom I quoted earlier, said,

> As to Campbellism, that spectre which haunts many good men and terrifies them into a good deal of bad interpretation, shall we gain anything by maintaining a false translation and allowing the Campbellites to be champions of the true, with the world's scholarship on their side as against us?[1]

All lovers of truth should rejoice when men like Mr. Willmarth respect scholarship and truth above any party. In spite of party spirit, such men are big enough in soul to give true interpretations of God's Word. . . .

Peter taught penitent believers to be baptized so that sins might be blotted out. . . . I am certain that one may be a Christian—only a Christian—and believe this same doctrine; for Peter was a Christian—only a Christian—and he believed and taught it. I am indeed glad whenever any group or teacher endorses this undenominational teaching. Such teaching heartily agrees, at this point, with the biblical teaching of those who are striving to be just Christians and who belong to no denomination, but simply were added to the church of God by the Lord at the time they were saved. How glad I would be to see all honest hearts be undenominational in all their teaching! If any sincere believer in Christ will

---

[1] James W. Willmarth, in *Baptist Quarterly* (July 1877): 304–5.

accept the obvious interpretation and teach baptism as immersion, he may be "of one heart and soul" with every undenominational Christian in the world.

Are we really ready to give up "parties," "sects," and denominationalism to become Christians only? Are we ready to do all we can to make God's children one? Remember that, to be an undenominational preacher, one must preach that Peter commanded baptism unto, or, in order to receive, remission of sins. In so teaching, he is advocating not man's doctrine, but Christ's doctrine. He who names this doctrine as anything other than the teaching of Christ misrepresents Christ and His doctrine. Christ has stained this teaching with His own blood; therefore, it is His, and He is due all honor from it.

10

Undenominational Christianity— Explanation Needless

The word in Peter's speech that declares baptism to be "in order to" receive remission, or forgiveness, of sins (Acts 2:38) is as definite in meaning, as clear of ambiguity, as the English words "unto" and "into." No doubt, everyone in Peter's vast audience understood that he was offering salvation from sins on the conditions of repentance and baptism. Not one of them could have misunderstood the meaning. For Peter to have made the word *eis* mean "because of" or "in token of" would have been to give it a new meaning, a meaning never given it before or since by a Greek. Not only did every person in that vast audience understand Peter's unequivocal speech, but for hundreds of years following this undenominational meeting at Jerusalem, no student of the language, I suppose, ever failed to see that Peter was offering those inquiring souls pardon on those two conditions. We could venture the assertion that every teacher of the language, for many hundreds of years, so taught it.

The fact that the language was given one meaning for so many years is strong proof of the correctness of the interpretation. Its accuracy is especially supported by the fact that this interpretation is in harmony with the interpretation given by the best scholars today....

One may be a member of a denomination and not believe and teach this Bible doctrine. However, can he be simply a Christian—an undenominational Christian, a Christian like Peter—and not believe and teach what the Bible says?

We have dwelt on the work done in this meeting at Jerusalem because our Lord desires that His followers speak the same truths and that they be perfectly joined together in the same mind and in the same judgment. There is no just reason for division concerning these important matters dealt with at Jerusalem. If we divide into parties over them, it is inexcusable in us and shows us to be unfaithful to our Lord. We have especially dwelt upon the purpose of baptism as taught in this first meeting conducted by the inspired apostles guided by the Spirit, fresh from heaven, because true, honest hearts have made a "fork" in the road at this place and have separated. While there is no biblical reason for division here, there is perhaps some clear excuse for the division.

All true hearts hold that sinners must be taught of Jesus and shown that He is the Savior of men, that He died for them and arose again, and that He has been crowned King of kings and Lord of lords. These true hearts also agree that this knowledge of the crucified and risen Lord must so reach the hearts of the unsaved that they will be convicted of sins and realize their lost condition. Loyal hearts also agree that these believing, convicted hearts should repent—that is, reject their former lifestyles, turning away from sins—and, with a full purpose of heart and will to follow Jesus as Lord, surrender to Him in the divine commandment of baptism. It is agreed, too, that this faith held by unsaved souls, coupled with godly sorrow that leads to repentance, develops into a confiding and trusting dependence upon Jesus for salvation. Repentance is agreed to be the result of knowing "assuredly" that Jesus is Lord and Christ. Through the godly sorrow and repentance produced by knowledge of Christ, the soul comes into a state of reliance upon, and trust in, God our Father and the Lord Jesus Christ. Such a soul is a "given-up" spirit and, like Saul of Tarsus, says, "What shall I do, Lord?" (Acts 22:10). This "given-up," contrite, broken spirit is a truly converted soul, ready to do anything the Lord wants.

What more shall we say? Shall true hearts, loyal to Jesus, agreed thus far, separate into parties on the subject of baptism? How can they, while Jesus begs them to have no divisions among them? To just such souls as described above, Peter said, "Repent ye, and be baptized every one of you in the name of Jesus Christ unto the remission of your sins . . ." (Acts 2:38b). Ananias said to Saul, when his spirit was "given up" and he was fully surrendered to the Lord, "Arise, and be baptized, and wash away thy sins, calling on his name" (Acts 22:16b). Are we willing to say to other "given-up" spirits—souls that by faith, godly sorrow, and repentance have come into a state of reliance upon God and Christ—exactly what the inspired teachers said to such souls, and leave it at that?

Are you afraid that you will lose your party? Do

you love your party better than you love the union of saints? Would you rather hold to your party than to please Jesus? I am willing to present to the contrite, broken, surrendered spirit the very words of the Holy Spirit concerning his duty pertaining to baptism. I am willing to risk that he will understand it. For many hundreds of years, not one soul failed, so far as we know.

Do you hold to a theory that depends upon a complex explanation of simple words? The only excuse for division here is devotion to denominationalism. Christians can never be one, Jesus can never be pleased, and His prayer can never be answered in and through denominationalism. We must choose between the two. "Choose you this day whom ye will serve" (Joshua 24:15b). Loyal hearts will have to give up denominationalism. To be a Christian—just a Christian, nothing more and nothing less—is the greatest opportunity set before human hearts.

Undenominational Christianity—Baptism into What?

While we have dwelt on Peter's teaching in the first undenominational meeting, when the gospel was introduced on the Day of Pentecost, we have not done so because it is the only teaching on the subject. There are even plainer passages, if that is possible, than the one in Acts 2. We have dwelt on the teaching done in that first meeting because it was the first work the Holy Spirit did in guiding the inspired apostles into all truth.

We must examine carefully the original teaching on the much-disputed topic of baptism. All honest hearts need to see that there is no reason for division over the matter. We will see if Peter offered at this meeting remission, or forgiveness, of sins on the conditions of knowing assuredly that Jesus was made both Lord and Christ, of repentance, and of baptism. Surely, this should settle the discussion regarding Heaven's conditions of pardon to a lost sinner. Especially, this should settle the question since these teachers were commanded to go into all the world to preach repentance and remission of sins among all nations beginning at Jerusalem (Acts 1:8) and since they were clothed with power from heaven. Jesus had told them to "tarry" till that divine power came to guide them in their work, so that the work might be infallibly correct (Luke 24:46–49). If these teachers obeyed the orders of their Lord—if they waited at Jerusalem till the Holy Spirit came to guide them and then began at Jerusalem (none of which should be doubted)—then the work is absolutely correct and cannot be wrong.

If Peter offered remission of sins, the very thing he was sent to do, then surely he gave the conditions on which forgiveness could be obtained. If the Spirit, therefore, offered pardon to convicted hearts on the conditions of repentance and baptism at this meeting at Jerusalem, then this is Heaven's will and teaching. That is why we have dwelt on this work. Peter did, under the direct guidance of the Holy Spirit, command people to be baptized so that they might be forgiven. That truth is as certain as the fact that he spoke at all, the scholars of the world being the interpreters of the language. I have labored diligently to make this stand out clearly to every honest heart. Nothing but rebellion will separate hearts concerning the matter after a diligent examination of the language.

Now that it is settled as to what Peter taught in that first meeting, I must ask, Is this clear teaching of Peter in harmony with all teaching of the Spirit on the subject? To ask this question is to answer it. Peter could not have been a faithful teacher of remission of sins if his teaching had conflicted with the teaching of the Spirit at any point. Therefore, his teaching at Jerusalem must harmonize with all other teachings of the Spirit.

Just before this meeting at Jerusalem, Peter and the other apostles were given orders from the Master concerning this great work. Peter was carrying out these orders in this meeting at Jerusalem. What were their orders? According to Matthew's record, they were as follows:

> All authority hath been given unto me in heaven and on earth. Go ye therefore, and make disciples of all the nations, baptizing them into [*eis*] the name of the Father and of the Son and of the Holy Spirit: teaching them to observe all things whatsoever I commanded you: and lo, I am with you always, even unto the end of the world (Matthew 28:18–20).

These were the orders as Matthew recorded them; and if Peter did not observe them on the Day of Pentecost, then he was an unfaithful teacher. If he taught anything concerning baptism that was not in harmony with these orders, we should reject Peter as an inspired teacher.

On the contrary, at this first meeting on the Day of Pentecost, Peter *did* teach the listeners about Jesus, His life, His death, His resurrection, and His coronation at the right hand of the Father. He called upon them to know assuredly that God had made the crucified Jesus both Lord and Christ. Without doubt, those who then knew all this about Jesus had been made disciples, or learners, of Jesus. According to the divine orders, however, after making disciples, the apostles were to baptize these disciples "into" something. Evidently, before their baptism these disciples had not entered that something, whatever it may have been. Otherwise, these holy preachers of the gospel could not have baptized them "into" it.

Again, I ask for careful consideration here, because everything depends upon slow and faithful deliberation. These are our Lord's everlasting orders on earth. Whatever these disciples were to be baptized "into" is the thing "into" which every disciple is to be baptized, and he can't possibly get "into" that thing without baptism. What was the something "into" which Peter and others were to baptize disciples? The divine command referred to "baptizing them into the name of the Father and of the Son and of the Holy Spirit." Before baptism, the disciples made by these preachers were out of the name of the Father and of the Son and of the Holy Spirit, but they entered into it by baptism. Can one be in the family of God, a child of God, while he is out of the "name" of the family? Can he be an heir of the Father's blessings without putting on the family name, the Father's name?

Imagine two young people being joined in marriage. The young man's name is Jones, and the young lady's name is Smith. This young lady loves the young man and has, perhaps, for months; but they are not yet married. She is still Miss Smith; but by a few words spoken in a wedding ceremony, she is married to the young man. By the same means and at the same time, she passes "into" the father's and son's name; ever after, her name is "Jones." She enters the name "Jones" and is an heiress to the Jones estate. Just so, the apostles were sent into the world to lead sinners to be joined with Christ so that they might be "married to another, even to him who is raised from the dead" (Romans 7:4; KJV), so that they might bring forth fruit unto God. When were they married to Christ: before entering the name of Father and Son, or at the entering of it? When did they enter the family, God's family: before marrying the Son, or at the marriage? Matthew 28:19 says, ". . . baptizing them into the name of the Father and of the Son and of the Holy Spirit." Who can doubt that these who were made disciples of Jesus according to the divine orders were to become children of the God-family by being baptized into the divine name?

On the Day of Pentecost, Peter, under these orders, told believing, sorrowing, penitent hearts, new disciples of Christ, to be baptized "unto" (*eis*) the remission of sins. He used the very same word that our Savior used in giving the orders, indicating specifically that "unto" which, or "into" which, they were to be baptized.

The only difference in the phrasing is the object following the word *eis*. In the orders given by Christ, the apostles were to baptize believers "into" the great name of God; in Peter's language, they were baptized "unto" the remission of sins. Who can doubt, then, that the soul surrendered to Christ with a full purpose of heart is baptized "into" the name of the Father, the Son, and the Holy Spirit and is also baptized "unto" remission of sins? In truth, he could not be baptized "unto" the one without entering "into" the other. They are not identical purposes, but "into the name of the Father and of the Son and of the Holy Spirit" is the great, comprehensive, divine relationship entered by baptism; it includes all the blessings found in that relationship. No one can be baptized "into" the name of the Father, the Son, and the Holy Spirit without at the same moment being baptized "unto" remission of sins and "unto" all other blessings of that divine relationship.

Therefore, Peter, on the Day of Pentecost, in dealing with the murderers of our Lord whose hearts were bowed down with heavy grief for this special sin and who were crying for relief from it, told them to be baptized "unto" (*eis*) the remission of their sins. This was the thing for which they were longing, crying, sighing, and seeking. Peter gave them a specific answer; but if he had told them to be baptized "into the name of the Father and of the Son and of the Holy Spirit," their humble obedience to this command would have brought them "unto" remission of sins. Such forgiveness is but one of the blessings found by all who enter that divine relationship.

At Ephesus, Paul found about twelve men who had been baptized "into John's baptism" (Acts 19:3), evidently after it had ceased to be a divine ordinance. They had been taught to believe that Jesus was still to come; they had been baptized looking for Him when, in fact, He had already come, had already died, and had risen from the grave years before Paul's visit to Ephesus. To be sure, they had been baptized "unto" the remission of sins, for John's baptism was a "baptism of repentance unto remission." However, their baptisms had been prompted by faith in a coming Lord, when it should have been in a crucified and risen Lord. They were ignorant of the great facts of the gospel of Christ; they did not know that He had been exalted to the right hand of God to be a real Savior, "to give repentance to Israel, and remission of sins." Therefore, Paul taught them these great facts and commanded them to be baptized "into [*eis*] the name of the Lord Jesus" (Acts 19:5).

Did Paul's command to these men differ materially from Peter's answer to the three thousand penitent believers at Jerusalem? "In none other [than Christ] is there salvation: for neither is there any other name under heaven, that is given among men, wherein we must be saved" (Acts 4:12). Peter told the three thousand to be baptized "unto" (*eis*) remission; since there is remission, or salvation, in no other name, it follows that Peter was virtually commanding them to be baptized into that name by which we must be saved. Since salvation is in no other name and Peter said to be baptized unto remission, or salvation, his answer implied their entrance into that name. Salvation is "in" the name of the Lord Jesus and not "out of" it; neither is it "in" any other name. These people were baptized so that they might be saved, which required that they be placed "in" Christ.

I beg permission to say again that honest hearts cannot separate here. There can be no division if we want the union for which Jesus prayed. I am willing to use the Spirit's own words to cry out to the believing, penitent heart, to the one with the broken will and contrite spirit, to the one crying, "What shall I do, Lord?" (Acts 22:10):

> [Be baptized] into the name of the Father and of the Son and of the Holy Spirit (Matthew 28:19).

> Be baptized every one of you in the name of Jesus Christ unto the remission of your sins

(Acts 2:38).

[Be] baptized into the name of the Lord Jesus (Acts 19:5).

Arise, and be baptized and wash away thy sins, calling on his name (Acts 22:16).

I am willing to set these words before him without explanation, leaving his heart to understand the answer, risking that he will understand the Spirit's clear instructions.

Are you afraid that your denomination will suffer without an explanation of the words "into" and "unto"? Are you unwilling to sacrifice your denominationalism, if quoting and following the very words of God's Book eliminates it? Are you content to be a Christian only—nothing more and nothing less, just such a Christian as New Testament Christians were? Is it not enough to be a plain humble follower of the Man of Galilee? Since there were no denominational Christians in New Testament times, can you think of any biblical reason why there should be now?

Denominationalism forever hinders the prayer of the Savior that all who believe on Him may be one, as He and the Father are one (John 17:11). Our Lord entreats that there be no divisions among us, but that we all speak the same things and that we be perfectly joined together in the same mind and in the same judgment (1 Corinthians 1:10). His will can never be obeyed so long as such divisions exist. Why not be just a Christian for Christ's sake?

Undenominational Christianity— Baptized into What?

The word "into" is so well known to English-speaking people that it hardly seems necessary to dwell upon its meaning in an effort to make it clearer. Nevertheless, at the risk of being tedious, I want to call special attention to its definitely fixed meaning. It may help some soul to a clearer view of the truth; if so, we can afford to weary others for the sake of this one.

Let us illustrate the use of this word. If someone announced to a mother that her baby had fallen "into" the well, the mother would know exactly where the baby was; she would run immediately and would never stop until she came to that well. Every effort would be made to get the baby "out" of the well. Likewise, if it were announced on good authority that a thief had gone "into" a house, the police officer would not look for him on the outside. If a son told his father that the mules had jumped "into" the cornfield, without further explanation the father would understand that the mules had jumped "out of" the field or pasture where they were intended to stay and had entered "into" the cornfield.

So well fixed and so definite is the meaning of "into" that all of us always "see," or understand, it alike. In every use of it, we assume a passing "out of" something "into" something else. When the mules jumped "into" the corn, they were compelled to jump "out of" whatever they were in before. This is an absolute necessity, and every person so "sees" it in this way and agrees to this use. Every reader would be perfectly united with every other one on the meaning of "into" in such sentences. It is absolutely impossible to misunderstand its meaning. I would be interested to see someone attempt to construct an English sentence containing the simple word "into" which, upon interpretation, could lead to a misunderstanding of the word "into" by two honest hearts.

Could a mule jump "into" a place when he is already in that place? Could a baby fall "into" a well when it is already in that well? Can anything pass "into," jump "into," fall "into," or in any other way enter a place without first being on the outside of that place? Can a young lady enter the marriage relationship after she is already married? Before she is married, she is out of the relationship; but on marrying she passes "into" that relationship and remains afterward "in" that relationship.

Now, with this clearly defined meaning of "into," I ask honest hearts to examine some clear passages from the Holy Spirit:

> Go ye therefore, and make disciples of all the nations, baptizing them into the name of the Father and of the Son and of the Holy Spirit (Matthew 28:19).

> And when they heard this, they were baptized into the name of the Lord Jesus (Acts 19:5).
>
> Or are ye ignorant that all we who were baptized into Christ Jesus were baptized into his death? (Romans 6:3).
>
> For in one Spirit were we all baptized into one body (1 Corinthians 12:13a).
>
> For as many of you as were baptized into Christ did put on Christ (Galatians 3:27).

Therefore, in New Testament times, holy men of God, moved by power from on high, baptized people "into" (*eis*) the name of the Father and of the Son and of the Holy Spirit. They baptized them "into" (*eis*) the name of the Lord Jesus. They baptized them "into" (*eis*) Christ. They baptized them "into" (*eis*) Christ's death. They baptized them "into" (*eis*) one body. They baptized them "into" (*eis*) Christ; thus those being baptized put Him on. Finally, the apostles baptized people "unto" or "into" (*eis*) the remission of their sins.

If we give the word "into" in these passages its unequivocal meaning, then there can be no misunderstanding. People in New Testament times, before their baptism, were "out of" the name of the Father, and of the Son, and of the Holy Spirit, were "out of" Christ's death, were "out of" the one body, were "out of" Christ, and were "away from" the remission of sins. By baptism, they entered these holy and divinely created relationships and blessings.

Therefore, whatever blessings are to be had by entering the holy names, by entering Christ's death, by entering the holy body of Christ, by entering Christ Himself, and by coming unto the remission of sins are dependent upon scriptural baptism. This must be so, or else language is not the proper instrument for the conveyance of thought, and we can rely upon nothing conveyed to us by the power of speech.

No wonder Ananias said to the weeping and mourning Saul of Tarsus, "... arise, and be baptized, and wash away thy sins, calling on his name" (Acts 22:16). No wonder Peter said, "... wherein few, that is, eight souls, were saved through water: which also after a true likeness doth now save you, even baptism..." (1 Peter 3:20, 21a).

Indeed, how could holy men have taught otherwise? Jesus, in giving His last and final orders, had said, "Go ye into all the world, and preach the gospel to the whole creation. He that believeth and is baptized shall be saved; but he that disbelieveth shall be condemned" (Mark 16:15, 16). If Jesus and the inspired apostles have not taught that the properly prepared heart is saved in and at the completion of the act of scriptural baptism, then it cannot be done by human speech.

Once more, I appeal to honest hearts. How can we make a "fork" in the road, dividing into parties concerning the relationship of baptism to salvation, or remission of sins, when the Holy Spirit has been so plain and clear in the matter? Our blessed Lord entreats us to speak the same things, to have no divisions among us, but to be perfectly joined together in the same mind and in the same judgment. How true and loyal hearts can continue loyal to Jesus and separate into divisions over unequivocal teaching of the Holy Spirit is beyond my understanding. How they can claim to be loyal and continue in division is more than I can see. When divisions are purposely encouraged and continued in the face of our Lord's clear and unequivocal teaching, wickedness and sin are surely crouching at the door.

Again, I plead with all who are willing to give up "parties," "theories," and denominationalism to be content and glad to be only Christians—just such Christians as Peter, James, and John were. Let us be just such Christians as all the members of the church at Jerusalem were—just such Christians as all Christians were in New Testament times. May the earnest prayer of the dying Savior again be a reality! Who among us is willing to give up anything and everything not required by the Holy Spirit so that we may be one for Jesus' sake? This unity would please our Lord; and through it, the lost world might believe that God sent Him. Is this not enough to move true hearts to oneness in Christ?

Undenominational Christianity— Another Fork

In this discussion of undenominational Christianity, we have come to another "fork" in the road where honest hearts have divided. Some believe that baptism may be sprinkling, pouring, or immersion and that one may submit to any of these acts and be scripturally baptized. While I would not question for a moment the sincerity of these hearts or their honest intentions, I am certain that they are mistaken. I am just as sure that God has made Himself so plain in this matter that honest hearts must agree after a fair and careful examination of the Holy Spirit's language. "God is not mocked" (Galatians 6:7), and He entreats us to be one; therefore, we may be one if we will.

Since we are driven by the language of the Holy Spirit to the conviction that baptism is a divine condition of pardon, we would do well to search diligently for its meaning so that we may obey our Lord. It is important, since every truly converted heart wants to obey the Master, to make it his daily "aim . . . to be well-pleasing unto him" (2 Corinthians 5:9). It is important, too, because every loyal heart wants to be one with every other true believer. Certainly, we can never speak the same things and be perfectly joined together in the same mind and in the same judgment while one teaches that baptism is sprinkling and another teaches that it can be only immersion. If our hearts are right with God, if we want to please Christ, then we will be anxious to know just what our Lord means by the words "baptism" and "baptize," and we will never be content till we do know His real meaning. Hence, let us make a careful and fair examination of the word used by our Lord.

When I was a child, my teachers taught me that words are signs of ideas and that ideas are mental pictures. If this is correct, then two people who understand the meaning of a word see the same picture in that word. For example, suppose I should write on the blackboard before a class of ten children the word "cow." If these children knew the meaning of "cow," then they would see in the word a picture of an animal, a cow. Each one would get the same kind of picture. If one of them saw in the word a sheep while another saw a pig and still another saw a chicken, all of them would miss the meaning. Think of the word "jump." Suppose one child saw the action of running, another saw walking, and still another pictured the action of creeping. Again, all three would miss the meaning.

Suppose I should order from a "mail-order" business a chair, but the man who supplied my order saw in the word "chair" a rug instead. What would be the result? Certainly, I would receive a rug instead of a chair. Suppose I wanted to order a pig from a livestock

UNDENOMINATIONAL CHRISTIANITY— ANOTHER FORK

breeder, but on the order I happened to write "rooster." What would the man send me? A rooster, of course. The whole business world would be ruined in a week by practicing the doctrine "We can't see alike." Men thousands of miles apart are engaged in daily business, buying and selling goods, without misunderstanding an order, because they *do* understand exactly alike. Why may not these same men do business with Heaven and understand God's words alike?

Jesus used the word "baptize." This is an action word; to get the meaning, we must see the action that Jesus desired to set forth. Whenever we see the correct action, we shall see alike. This is certainly possible unless Jesus used an ambiguous word; and in that case, Jesus Himself would be responsible for the disagreement in the world over the action of baptism.

What does His word mean? The word "baptize" is a Greek term, having never been translated at all, but made English only in form (Anglicized). Since the term is Greek and not English, we must go to the Greek dictionary rather than an English one to get its meaning. Any Greek teacher will endorse the statement that the word has been lifted out of the Greek language into the English without translation, having had performed on it only the process of substituting corresponding letters to make the word English in form (transliteration). This being true, it is evident that we must get from the word the idea or picture that the Greeks saw in it.

"Baptism" was not a new word, but an old one; it had been used by the Greeks without change of meaning for hundreds of years. If, at the time in which Jesus used this word, it had been written on a chalkboard before a thousand Greeks, every one of them would have been perfectly united on the meaning, "seeing it alike." They would have seen as nearly the same picture of "baptism" as a thousand English-speakers would see today in the word "cow." The Savior's word was that definite.

W. W. Goodwin, author of *Goodwin's Greek Grammar*, in a letter to J. W. Shepherd dated July 27, 1893, said of "baptize" (Gk: *baptizo*), "I have no knowledge about *baptizo* which you will not find in the ordinary lexicons. It means dip—a form of *bapto*, and I am not aware of anything peculiar in its use." Liddell and Scott's Greek dictionary says, *"baptizo*: (1) to dip in or under water. . . . (2) to draw wine by dipping the cup in the bowl."

Sophocles' definition was *"baptizo . . .* to dip, to immerse: to sink." J. H. Thayer wrote, *"baptizo*: (1) prop., to dip repeatedly, to immerge, submerge." With these eminent scholars agrees practically the entire scholarship of the world. No scholar has ever given, as a meaning of *baptizo* (or "baptize"), "sprinkle" or "pour." This means that no scholar, in all of his searching and researching of Greek literature, has found one occurrence of this word where it meant "sprinkle" or "pour." It never was used by a Greek with either one of these meanings. To demonstrate this, we may cite the living fact that the Greek church has never practiced "sprinkling" or "pouring" for baptism. Though that church practices infant baptism, it has always immersed its babies. Actually, the word was as definitely fixed among Greeks as "dip" is in our language. An English speaker could see the act of sprinkling in the word "dip" as easily as a Greek could see it in *"baptizo."*

Not only are all scholars and the Greek people a unit respecting the definition of the word used by our Savior, but the whole English-speaking world is one on the meaning of "baptize" as an English word. Should hundreds of school children in St. Louis go home tomorrow afternoon and say, "Our teachers baptized us with work," every parent would understand the same thought. Should the thousands of readers of the *Dallas News* read tomorrow, "Mr. Jones on Park Street is baptized in debt," not one would fail to understand that Mr. Jones was much in debt—that he was overwhelmed with debt. Not one intelligent reader would believe that the man mentioned owed only a few small payments. We would "see it alike." It is good English to say "baptized in trouble," "baptized in work," "baptized with sufferings," and so forth. No English reader would fail to see the meaning of "baptize" in such an expression, nor would there be any division concerning its meaning.

Does this word have one meaning in English and another meaning in the English Bible? Why do we see it alike in the *Dallas News* but divide over its meaning in our Lord's teaching? Let honest hearts ponder well before answering. There is absolutely no reason for the division in the religious world over the action of baptism. If we would be one, we could be. There is nothing to prevent it but the love for individual parties, even denominationalism.

Undenominational Christianity— What Is Baptism?

The purpose of this study is to lead every honest soul to see that divisions among believers are wrong, that they are contrary to the will of our Father through Christ, and that Christ and His apostles prayed and worked for the oneness of believers. To be Christian—like Christ—every Christian must therefore condemn these divisions and strive earnestly to keep the unity of the Spirit in the bond of peace. (See John 17:20, 21; Acts 4:32; 1 Corinthians 1:10–13; Ephesians 4:1–6.)

The faithful and loyal in heart need to realize that denominationalism is the very source of these divisions. To belong to a denomination is to support it; no one can be a member of a denomination without directly setting his life against the plainest of Bible teaching. If we are ever to do away with the evil of division among believers, we must sweep all denominationalism off the earth.

A strict adherence to the Word of God would obliterate and eliminate every principle of denominationalism from present-day teaching. He who is guided only by the Holy Spirit in his religious life can be only a Christian, a disciple of the Lord, a child of God. For hundreds of years—including the hundred years in which Jesus, the apostles, and hundreds of other inspired men lived—no believer in Christ was known by any name other than such as those designations given above. Then where did denominationalism originate? Into which church did holy men of God lead people? In what church did Christians in the days of inspiration live, work, and worship? Nobody claims that any one of the denominational churches existed then. It is more certain than death that, according to the entire New Testament history, there were only churches of God, churches of Christ. Only to these did the Holy Spirit write. Not one single line of instruction is given in all the New Testament to any denominational church. Certainly, the Holy Spirit could not have written to that which did not exist. One can find instructions in the New Testament to the Masonic Lodge, to the Woodmen of the World, or to the government of the United States as easily as he can find instructions to any denomination.

By irrefutable logic, it follows that those who faithfully observe the Holy Spirit's teaching as given in the New Testament must be Christians only. Following biblical truth in their teachings and in their lives makes them nothing but members of the church of God. No one can deny this.

A faithful effort has been made in this study to show that we may "see" alike. At least, we can see so nearly alike that the beautiful flower of union planted in God's garden in the first century may grow unmolested and unhurt in the twenty-first century. Believers living in this century may be of one heart and one soul as truly as were the disciples in the first century. The teaching of the Holy Spirit is so plain that there is no excuse, save love and devotion to denominationalism, for division over His plain guidance.

In our examination of the first meeting held after the apostles' "waiting" for guiding power, we have found two points of doctrine at which true hearts have divided. On a thorough examination of Peter's language, however, it has been shown that there is no scriptural reason for division of true hearts at the first "fork" in the road. To let Peter's language have its ordinary and obvious meaning destroys the wicked division that has been made there and unites every heart in Christ without the sacrifice of a single truth. The scholarship of the world serves as judge, affirming that this simplest interpretation is the best.[1] At this point, it only remains to be seen how many hearts are willing to give up all but the teaching of God so that oneness in Christ may be established.

In the previous chapter, we were examining the second "fork" in the road. This "fork" has been made over the action of baptism. There are good, true hearts in the world who believe in Jesus. Through that faith, they have been brought to godly sorrow; and, through deep

---

[1] Review chapter 8, "Undenominational Christianity—Saved After Baptism," and chapter 9, "Undenominational Christianity—Remission of Sins." Peter said that penitent believers must be baptized "unto" (*eis*) the remission of their sins, indicating that the obedient believer is forgiven only *after* baptism.

contrition of heart, they have deeply resolved to repudiate a life of sin (repented) and determined to live a life of righteousness. Nevertheless, by unscriptural teaching, they have been led to accept "sprinkling" or "pouring" for baptism. Thus they have failed to complete, many of us believe, the commandment of our Lord that requires one to be baptized. Be it far from me to question the sincerity of these hearts. I grant them the same honesty that I claim for my own heart; but honest hearts, fair hearts, must accept that equally sincere hearts have lived and been wrong, been mistaken. Since Jesus earnestly pleads for us all to be one, and since we can never be one while we thus disagree concerning what baptism is, it will benefit us to examine carefully, honestly, and fairly all that God has said on the subject.

The previous chapter referred to the fact that our word "baptize" is an Anglicized form of the Greek word used by our Lord. It is not a translation of the Greek word but is only a transposition of the word out of one language into another by simply changing its form enough to make it English in form and pronunciation. There is no dispute here. It was also contended in the previous chapter that this fact forces us to Greek dictionaries for the word's meaning. We must see the same picture in the word that the Greeks saw in it when Jesus used it. This is self-evident, unless Jesus was using it with a new meaning. This, no one claims. Anyone who will take the pains to investigate may satisfy himself thoroughly that all standard lexicographers of the Greek language are so nearly a unit in their definitions of this word that two honest hearts have to agree as to its meaning. No standard Greek-English lexicon (dictionary) ever gave "sprinkle" or "pour" as a meaning of the word. Liddell and Scott, in one edition of their lexicon, did give "pour upon"; but when they revised it, they eliminated this meaning, left it out. By so doing, they, too, have given their testimony that no Greek writer so far as we know ever used the word with the meaning "pour upon." It is entirely safe to say that no scholar would risk his scholarship in defense of "sprinkle" or "pour" as the meaning of the Greek word used by our Master in His command to us to be baptized.

If scholarship can settle anything as to the meanings of words, it has settled the meaning of *baptizo* ("baptize"), the word used by our Savior. According to this scholarship, the word from Homer's time forward has had one unvarying meaning. "To dip, immerse, plunge, overwhelm, submerge, wash" is the meaning given and endorsed by the world's scholarship.

Aside from the meaning of *baptizo* as a Greek word, the English word for it, "baptize," is given by English writers the same meaning that Greek-English lexicons give to the Greek word. Excluding for the moment its usage in religious writings, let us study it purely from an English view, determining its meaning from its use in "secular" English. In this way, we shall find that it means "submerge, overwhelm, plunge, immerse" or some equivalent. No secular passage can be found in which the word "baptize" occurs with a meaning equivalent to "sprinkle" or "pour." That is, no standard English writer ever used the word "baptize" other than to convey the meaning of immersing, plunging, overwhelming, or submerging the thing baptized. Being baptized involves being completely in or with the element employed. It is not an uncommon usage to find in English writings phrases like "baptized in debt," "baptized with work," "baptized with questions," "baptized in suffering," and so forth. In every one of these expressions, much of the element indicated is employed; the one baptized is overwhelmed, or submerged, in it or by it. No one gets any other idea of it.

It seems that the Lord has placed in my hand, to aid in this discussion, a most telling illustration of the meaning of this word in English. It was used in a well-written article printed in an issue of *Pictorial Review*. The article was the last installment of "The Love Letters of a Confederate General." In the last of these remarkable letters, the author, General George E. Pickett, wrote,

> It is finished—the suffering, the horrors, the anguish of these last hours of struggle of these men, *baptized in battle* at Bull Run, in the lines at Yorktown, at Williamsburg where they, with the Alabama Brigade of Wilcox, withstood advance of the whole of McClellan's army, driving them back at Seven Pines, Gaines' mill, Frazier's farm, Second Manassas, Boonsboro, Sharpsburg, Gettysburg, in the engagement in front of Bermuda Hundred, Fort Harrison, Five Forks and Sailor's Creek. (Emphasis added.)

Thousands of readers have read this article, and every reader surely understands "baptized in battle" exactly alike. All understand it to mean that these Civil War soldiers were overwhelmed in, or by, battle. The thought that they engaged in light skirmishes at these

UNDENOMINATIONAL CHRISTIANITY—
WHAT IS BAPTISM?

places where they were "baptized in battle" has never been suggested to a single reader. Regardless of his religious convictions about our Lord's commandment, each reader understands it exactly as I do. So it is in every passage ever written by standard English authors. The author always means that much of the element is involved and that the thing baptized is submerged by it. All English readers understand it exactly alike, except in our Lord's teaching. When we come to His holy teachings, we put on our denominational glasses and see in the word "baptize" that which we see in it in no other English writing. We give it an entirely new meaning, a meaning we allow nowhere else. Is this fair? Will God excuse the English-speaking world?

Undenominational Christianity— The Bible Meaning

In our study of the word "baptize," we have learned that it is not a translation of the Greek word used by the Savior, but that it is the very word itself changed in ending so that it may be incorporated into the English tongue without translation. Why the great scholarship of an intelligent world has dealt with this word in such a way, only God knows. Certainly, this learning has not failed to translate it for the lack of knowledge of the word.

Perhaps it would be interesting to hear the story of the failure from the earliest English translation of the Scriptures. Why did translators not give us a simple Anglo-Saxon word for this Greek one? When the secrets of men's hearts are known and the reasons for their actions are written "on the wall" by the hand of Him who knows the hearts of all men, then we shall find, I suspect, that we have been burdened through all these years with this Greek-English word to protect denominationalism in the world. Just think of it: If we did have a translation of this word, we would read,

> He that believeth and is dipped, immersed, submerged, or overwhelmed, shall be saved.
>
> Why tarriest thou? Arise and be dipped, immersed, or submerged, and wash away thy sins.
>
> Go ye therefore, and make disciples of all the nations, dipping, immersing, or submerging them into the name of the Father.
>
> Repent, and be dipped, immersed, or submerged in the name of Jesus Christ unto the remission of your sins.

My, what exposure this would be to the doctrines that substitute "sprinkling" and "pouring" for baptism! What defense could be made for them? Is this why the word was not translated? Was it to save the doctrines and practices of great and popular peoples in the world that hold to pouring and sprinkling? Let honest hearts answer.

Nevertheless, God is wiser than men. He has far surpassed them in every race; He has defeated them in every battle. Though they have failed to give us a single translation of this word used by our Savior, God has not failed to make its meaning stand out so clearly that anyone who reads may understand. Thanks be to God that no step leading to the blood of our Lord is dependent upon the meaning of one word. This highway of life through Jesus has been made plain in various ways, so that men are without excuse. We may know His will, if we want to know it.

Suppose, now, that we did not know the certain fact that the word "baptize" is a Greek word, Anglicized. Suppose we had never heard of the Greek language and did not know that Jesus spoke any language other than English: Could we learn the meaning of this word and thus learn what to do in order to be baptized? Could one take the New Testament in English and be sure of his obedience? Most assuredly. The first man sent of Heaven to baptize was John the Baptist. It is possible, too, that he baptized more people than any other one man. This first baptizing of hundreds of souls was done in the historic Jordan River. Indeed, many people "were baptized of him in the river Jordan, confessing their sins" (Matthew 3:6). We also read, "Jesus came from Nazareth of Galilee, and was baptized of John in [*eis*; "into"] the Jordan. And straightway coming up out of the water, he saw the heavens rent asunder, and the Spirit as a dove descending upon him" (Mark 1:9, 10). Without doubt, then, the first baptizing was done "in a river"; people were baptized (*eis*) into the river. Jesus came up out of the water. Let the honest heart decide whether these facts are in harmony with "sprinkling," "pouring," or "immersion." Which could it be? God calls on you to decide. God has drawn pictures for you so that you may know how to obey Him.

Let us consider another example:

> And Philip opened his mouth, and beginning from this scripture, preached unto him

> Jesus. And as they went on the way, they came unto a certain water; and the eunuch saith, Behold, here is water; what doth hinder me to be baptized? And he commanded the chariot to stand still: and they both went down into the water, both Philip and the eunuch; and he baptized him (Acts 8:35–38).

This is the case of two men traveling on a lonely desert road. There is no crowd to obstruct our view of what was being done. The preacher, very intent on his duty, preached Jesus to his companion. As they continued their journey, the man preached to—not the preacher—beheld some water. In what seems to have been a very abrupt manner, he stopped the preacher and directed his attention to the water, asking that he might be baptized. The chariot was stopped, and both men got out of the chariot and went "down into the water." The eunuch was baptized, and they both—Philip and the eunuch—came "up out of the water." How long will the honest heart have to look upon this picture to see in it "sprinkling" or "pouring"? Can the heart intent on doing what God wants done, after watching this case directed by the Holy Spirit, be satisfied with "sprinkling" or "pouring"?

Let us look further, examining additional pictures of baptism given to us by God's Holy Spirit:

> ... are ye ignorant that all we who were baptized into Christ Jesus were baptized into his death? We were buried therefore with him through baptism into death ... (Romans 6:3, 4).

Having been buried with him in baptism, wherein ye were also raised with him through faith in the working of God, who raised him from the dead (Colossians 2:12).

Let us draw near with a true heart in fulness of faith, having our hearts sprinkled from an evil conscience: and having our body washed with pure water (Hebrews 10:22).

Paul said that he and all the Roman church had been "buried" through baptism. He also told the Colossians that they had been "buried" in baptism. John Wesley, the founder of the Methodist church, said that Paul in this passage from Romans was referring to the "ancient mode of baptizing by immersion." The writer of the Book of Hebrews depicted baptism as a washing.

Let us review and consider thoughtfully these facts connected with New Testament baptism:

1. The first baptizing was done in a river.
2. Jesus was baptized into the Jordan.
3. Jesus came up out of the water after His baptism.
4. Philip and the eunuch went down into the water.
5. While in the water, the eunuch was baptized.
6. Both Philip and the eunuch came up out of the water after the baptism.
7. Paul said that the entire church at Rome and also the congregation at Colossae, including himself, had been buried by, through, or in baptism.

8. All of the Hebrew brethren are said to have had their bodies washed with pure water.

Greek or no Greek, no honest heart can fail to see what New Testament preachers and teachers did when they were baptizing people. Remember that for thirteen hundred years immersion was the universal practice; anything else for baptism was denied. Since the entire Christian world for more than a thousand years was united on the action of baptism, it would be wise for someone to account for the changing of the practice. Surely, the whole world did not miss the meaning of the word for a thousand years; surely, inspired men were guided in their obedience to this commandment. I will leave the matter with the honest. May we be one on this mooted question? Jesus entreats it, the Holy Spirit pleads for it, and the entire teaching of the apostolic age demands it. Will we examine the truth and accept it, for Jesus' sake?

———◇———

This closes our study on "Undenominational Christianity." I hope it may do some good. In writing it, I have made no effort to display my learning or my logic, if I have either. I have had one aim, and that is to be plain and simple, so that the common reader may read the book without a dictionary. If I have been plain, if I have been simple, if I have been scriptural, then I am satisfied. I have no defense for the work otherwise. If critics desire to criticize it, let them criticize the lesson that I have proposed to teach.

I pray that God will use the truth taught in this study for the salvation of souls, for the uniting of His saints, and for the strengthening of His church wherever it is planted. When I am dead, I pray that it can be said of me, "He was a Christian," meaning that I was, in spirit, zeal, and courage, a real follower of the Christ; that I belonged to Him and only to Him; that I had no other ruler but Jesus; that my citizenship was in heaven; and that I was truly a sojourner and a foreigner on the earth. All of my efforts to do good, to prevent evil, to overcome wickedness, and to bless the world have been done through Him and by Him; it has been the purpose of my life to reproduce among men His holy life. If it may be said that I gave my life away in return for His blood, then I ask for no other monument.